Praise for

Living Your Values and *The Values Edge 2.0*

"Once again, Dennis Jaffe and Cynthia Scott have produced the premier set of tools for defining, prioritizing, and implementing values-based living and purposeful action. *Living Your Values* advances the work that advisors do by identifying and integrating both personal and shared values in the family ever more clearly. This step is often the missing link for families, since it requires deep discussion and difficult negotiation. A new chapter on values in organizations integrates the process for all businesses, whether family or nonfamily. Throughout the workbook, stories of real individuals and real companies bring the concepts to life. *Living Your Values* is truly a guidebook to creating a values-based life, family, business, and culture."

—Jim Grubman, PhD, co-author of *Strangers in Paradise* and *Wealth 3.0*

"*Living Your Values* provides the structure and framework for helping families find clarity about what they value most. It shows how values matter for individuals to set their life purpose and guides the family to create enterprise resilience across generations. As an advisor for many years, I have used The Values Edge 2.0 to help complex families find personal clarity to craft shared family values statements and build strong culture that allows them to steer through challenging family decisions. Cynthia and Dennis have provided the architecture and encouragement for families and their advisors to have one of the most important conversations families can have—how to become values-driven enterprises."

—Amy Hart Clyne, chief knowledge and learning officer, Pitcairn

"'Values.' A word that is used so frequently as to have lost much of its meaning and specificity. Yet values are the guiding light that define our decisions, our relationships and our definition of who we are. They are foundational to how we see the world and how the world sees us.

While Dennis Jaffe is well known for his work in helping families of means navigate their often-complex decisions and journeys, this book is not only for the wealthy. He, and Cynthia Scott, both behavioral science PhDs, have written a book of great value for any individual, any family, that values a deep dive into what it takes to make values a meaningful, vibrant, and foundational part of life. They never parrot simplistic ideas about values but underscore the work needed to actually align one's decisions with ones stated values.

This book is indispensable for individuals, community group, businesses and families who have the courage and the curiosity to take a deep and honest look at how successfully they are managing to 'live their values.' Highest recommendation."

—Madeline Levine, PhD, author of *The Price of Privilege*, *Teach Your Children Well*, and *Ready or Not*

"Wealth planning and heir preparation needs a foundation of shared family values to overcome the inevitable friction from difference in values about what the money is for. In my five years chairing two Tiger 21 groups, The Values Edge 2.0 is the best vehicle for quickly bringing to the surface areas where your family's values are aligned, and potential misalignments that could cause tension and conflict. Heirs and advisors in the family wealth use this to take the first step to understanding their current and aspirational values that the family wants to embody post liquidity."

—J.B. Bernstein, Las Vegas chair of Tiger 21

"Dennis and Cynthia's deep research on values is a superb way to stimulate reflective thinking and vibrant discussions. There are no easy answers to identifying what you most value and that's why it's powerful. You have to make choices and trade-offs. I use the Values Edge frequently in my talks and workshops and it always a hit. I've become a superfan!"

—<mark>Karen Dillon,</mark> Banyan Global Family Business Advisors, co-author of New York Times bestseller, *How Will You Measure Your Life?*

"As a senior advisor in a major financial institution, I have been using The Values Edge 2.0 toolkit for two years with global families. Clients value the simplicity of the process and find it enables both individual and families to generate valuable clarity, reduce conflict and increase alignment across generations. The gamification, and underlying framework of eight broad clusters has brought deep insight for clients to understand other family members values. I use the questions in the toolkit to help me deepen my approach to bringing clients attention to areas that will impact their future navigation and bring them powerful realization of directions for growth. I enjoy seeing my clients discover deep insights that impact their lives and direction for legacy generations."

—<mark>Asin Nurani,</mark> ultra-high-net-worth family governance advisor

"Articulation of family shared values and purpose is a foundation of my work with multigenerational families. While these values are within every person and every family, expressing them can be a challenge. Simplistic methods like surveys or asking people to pick from a list are too transactional and don't actually work. The Values Edge's 2.0 approach allows family members to apply a process that not just helps them understand their values but also acts as a conversation starter in the family group. The eight clusters add a dimension that gives family members further deep insights into themselves and the opportunity to find themes in common with others."

—<mark>Peter Begalla,</mark> founder and president, JPB Consulting Group, Inc

" The conversation about values is a complex and significant part of ensuring generational continuity. The Values Edge 2.0 provide a powerful way to deliver deeper, more meaningful, and ultimately more successful outcomes for my clients to identify, prioritize, and understand their foundational values in an easy and accessible way. "

—Richa Singh, senior consultant, Family Business Consulting Group

" The Values Edge 2.0 is one of my favorite tools for executives and teams strengthening their leadership capacity. Within minutes, team members begin reflecting on what matters most to them—both individually and collectively, setting a tone of openness, authenticity and energy for building a high-performing team. This process gives leaders an opportunity to reconnect with their core values—which may have drifted, it creates space for honest reflection and renewed focus, offering perspective on what truly matters across both personal and professional spheres. Clients consistently say how much they appreciate the tactile experience of the cards. In a world saturated by technology, this tool brings them back to something deeply human: being in touch with our core priorities, and commitments to ourselves and to others. Clients have called the experience 'a game changer' and 'a wake-up call'—refreshing their awareness to their values can spark real change—and action."

—Rebecca A. Turner, PhD, owner of Turner Consulting Group LLC

" Cynthia and Dennis have aggregated their research, practice, experience, and wisdom about values—and their impact on family resilience and flourishing—into a coherent, thoughtful, and invaluable work. All members of the family wealth and enterprise community will learn and benefit from this book. It places values where they need to be, at the core."

—Laurent Roux, CEO and founder of Gallatin Wealth Management LLC

"Dennis Jaffe and Cynthia Scott have been at the forefront of the defining and applying values in family business for decades. Their latest collaboration is a culmination of years of field-testing their ideas and refining their values-focused tools; it contains the deep wisdom of their rich professional experience. *Living Your Values* takes the reader on a learning journey of individual reflection and sparks conversations which reduce conflict. Whether you work in a family enterprise, want to elevate your family connectivity and relationships, or just want to bridge the gap between what you *aspire* to do and what you *do*, this book is the tool that will help you get there."

—Kristin Keffeler, chief learning officer, JFG Family Office, author of *The Myth of the Silver Spoon: Navigating Wealth & Creating an Impactful Life*, and co-author of *Wealth 3.0: The Future of Family Wealth Advising*

"I have found The Values Edge 2.0 accelerates the democratization—all voices get to be heard and seen. It kicks off the building a generative family through a fun, engaging, and visual process. Parents and rising generation members appreciate each family member differently adding depth to the family legacy stories. I use this process to kick-off a family council gathering, it lays the foundation for sharing stories and insights that shape a cohesive set of 'secret sauce' family values. Families say they 'know' their values but can't quite articulate them in a clear statement. Values Edge 2.0 has provided our client families confirmation of what needs to be cultivated and cherished as the family and enterprise moves through changes and challenges. We revisit The Values Edge 2.0 about every three to five years to refine and refresh their commitment."

—Dave Barnard, Barnard Family Wealth Group and RBC Dominion Securities

"*Living Your Values* consolidates the experience of how to use The Values Edge 2.0 with individuals, families and organizations. I have been using the Values Edge approach with clients for more than a decade. Most striking to me is the consistently quick engagement the tool engenders across multiple generations. Families have fun building and sharing their colorful values pyramids, which then leads to thoughtful and curious discussions of similarities and differences—sharing stories that lead to the development of a shared vision, focused philanthropy, governance and legacy direction."

—Patricia M. Armstrong, PhD, PMA Consulting,
Family Leadership Development

"The Values Edge 2.0 is an excellent tool to help our client family members identify their individual core values and establish shared family values statements to create a strong foundation in furtherance of their family legacy planning."

—Sisi Provost, director of family office services and
family education at Venturi Private Wealth

"Cynthia Scott and Dennis Jaffe are masters at helping families and organizations focus and live their values ... *Living Your Values* is an important book that will change lives."

—Barnaby Marsh, co-founder of Saint Partners and author of *How Luck Happens*

"As a psychologist working in the complex world of family wealth and enterprise, I've seen how values can either stay as abstract ideals or become powerful forces for real, lasting change. *Living Your Values* stands apart because it shows how to bring values to life—in action, in relationships, and in legacy. This framework has become central to how I help individuals, couples, and multigenerational families align their beliefs with their behaviors. it's a profoundly human roadmap that helps clients move toward what truly matters."

—Michele Mikeska Jaffe, executive director of family
wealth services, JPMorgan Wealth Management

"The Values Edge 2.0 gives couples a simple practical way to identify a prioritized set of core values and connect them to the behaviors that anchor those values. This approach creates a long-lasting conversation that blends current values and how they would like to focus their future. Using these tools s gives couples a way to visually sort out their identity and a framework to talk through important decisions and tensions that make a strong couple relationship."

—Marlis Jansen, LMFT, FBS, founder and CEO, Graddha LLC

"I use The Values Edge 2.0 in the early stages of work, to build the foundation of communication, purpose, and only then governance. Articulating a core set of values accelerates decisions and helps reduce perception of bias or secondary agendas in family decision-making, which is a common source of conflict. The training materials and workshop was extensive, and the team provides ongoing support to facilitators. Using this well-regarded platform helps me gain buy-in from the family into the values articulation process."

—David Werdiger, managing director, Nathanson Pearson Family Advisory

Cynthia D. Scott, PhD, MPH & Dennis T. Jaffe, PhD

Living Your
Values

Connecting Personal, Family, and Organizational Values
to Build Purpose and Clarity

**Family
Business
PRESS**

Published by Family Business Press
Austin, TX
www.rivergrovebooks.com

This work is being published under the *Family Business Press* imprint through an exclusive arrangement with *Family Business Magazine*. The *Family Business Magazine* and *Family Business Press* names, and the *Family Business Magazine* and *Family Business Press* logos, are wholly owned trademarks of *Family Business Magazine*.

Distributed by River Grove Books

Design and composition by Greenleaf Book Group and Brian Phillips
Cover design by Greenleaf Book Group and Brian Phillips

Publisher's Cataloging-in-Publication data is available.

Print ISBN: 978-1-968005-00-9

eBook ISBN: 978-1-968005-01-6

First Edition

To future generations,
may they use their values to inspire
and lead us wisely.

"This is the true joy in life, the being used for a purpose recognized by yourself as a mighty one . . . the being a force of Nature instead of a feverish, selfish little clod of ailments and grievances complaining that the world will not devote itself to making you happy."

—From *Man and Superman*, by George Bernard Shaw

"I am of the opinion that my life belongs to the whole community, and as long as I live, it is my privilege to do it for whatever I can. I want to be thoroughly used up when I die, for the harder I work, the more I live. I rejoice in life for its own sake. Life is no 'brief candle' to me. It is a sort of splendid torch which I've got a hold of for the moment, and I want to make it burn as brightly as possible before handing it on to future generations."

—From a speech by the playwright, featured in *George Bernard Shaw: His Life and His Works*, by Archibald Henderson

Contents

Living a Values-Enriched Life

Every day, each of us faces choices large and small in both our personal and professional lives: On the personal side, we may need to decide what groups to join, who to befriend, how to respond to slights and hurts, what causes to support, and whether to take on a challenge or try something new. In our business lives, we must decide whether we fit the organization we've joined (or whether to join an organization in the first place), what opportunities to pursue, and how to interact with our coworkers.

Many people choose spontaneously with little conscious reflection, rarely noticing their many choices or what criteria they use to choose between differing paths. Some spend lots of time over choices and always second-guess themselves; others follow their gut and move ahead with ease and flow.

But the people whom most of us tend to admire and want to emulate are those who live a life in which their choices and actions consistently reflect their stated beliefs. They are role models for the best of what a person can be. They use their values as the foundation for crafting who they are and what they become; they allow them to set goals, make decisions, and act. When values are manifested in someone's life, they feel whole and fulfilled, with a deep sense of purpose and goals to strive for.

It can be argued that what makes us human—the source of our power and capability as a species—is our unique ability to imagine and then make our dreams a reality. We are all magicians, able to conjure a new reality from our imagination. We also face new challenges and opportunities that invite us to move in new directions. It is human nature to have a vision of who and what we want to become and then feel driven to make sacrifices and expend energy toward those goals.

People who live close to their values are empowered by an internal fuel. They actively seek and discover new opportunities and relationships that align with those values. Defining values helps them narrow the gap between what they *want or aspire* to do and what they *actually* do. Bridging that gap is the purpose of this book.

Personal and Shared Values

Given how important values are, we owe it to ourselves to be aware of and thoughtful about what they are and how they operate in our lives. If our values remain unrecognized or unexplored, we miss the opportunity to reflect on what they are and use them to create resilience and focus. "Knowing thyself" begins with knowing your values and more importantly, working to live more fully according to them.

Making your personal values explicit helps you:

· express or refresh your life purpose and direction, including your career, family, and avocational paths.

· determine priorities for how you allocate your time, money, and resources.

· gather the courage to make difficult choices and change direction when life demands it.

· find freedom to enjoy change as it arises—wanted or unwanted.

- act in accordance with strong spiritual guidance.
- deepen self-knowledge and self-acceptance.

These benefits are important not just in helping us live more fulfilled lives but in helping us connect with others. We recognize that holding true to your personal values becomes challenging when you try to mesh them with those of others in any shared effort, such as a family or a business. In those cases, the group must articulate shared values in order to achieve smooth operations where the members can stay aligned through policies, practices, and governance. These shared values are often reinforced with stories of how they have brought success to the group.

Maintaining separation between an individual's personal values and the smaller set of shared group values makes it clear that an individual can have personal values not expressed in their family, team, or organizational realms. Differentiating between the two areas serves two purposes: (1) providing a respectful space for individuals to be responsible for expressing their personal values and (2) releasing a team, family, or organization from needing to be responsible for the fulfillment of all the values of the individuals who belong to the group.

Making Values Actionable

Identifying and acknowledging our values is just the first step. We have to push further to have our values manifest in our lives.

Most people would like to live more by their values, but they feel that their environment—other people, workplaces, and the community—can make this difficult. Sorting through these obstacles takes time and entails difficult choices, so many people try to avoid the resulting tug of a values conflict. This is an active and ongoing process.

Living Your Values is for any individual or group that wants to live a values-centered life, at a personal level and especially within a family or organization.

It provides a roadmap for individuals to easily define their personal values, and for families and teams to explore what they hold in common and how to work together more effectively. It is also useful for coaches, consultants, financial advisors, lawyers, and educators who are helping build strategies to bring greater meaning, purpose, and alignment for enhancing career, team, and organizational success and satisfaction and reducing inner and interpersonal conflict.

In this book, you'll find a guide to identifying, defining, clarifying, and living a life more fully according to your values. We have been translators of behavioral science research honed by decades of consulting with individuals, teams, families, and organizations seeking lives empowered by values and hoping to build more resilient and mission-driven enterprises.

We believe that for ideas and models to be useful, they must be practical and easy to use. One of the hallmarks of our books has been our ability to make our models clear, simple, and applicable to life and work. To accomplish that goal, *Living Your Values* provides not just discussion of key concepts, which you'll find in the main chapters, but also guided application exercises—in chapters labeled as **Learning Journeys**—that will help you apply the ideas to your own life. The tools we'll show you have proven useful for individuals, leaders, extended families, teams, startups, and multigenerational family businesses. Those processes and tools form the core of this book.

Part I, Chapters 1 to 4, is devoted to helping you clarify and define your personal values. Chapter 1 establishes a foundation for learning what values are and the roles they play in your life. Chapters 2 to 4 and their accompanying Learning Journeys go into more depth about how values shape your life. They focus on two key ideas:

- A practical model, called the **Values Wheel**, that will help you identify and shape your personal brand of individual, family, and organizational values.

- A tool called the **Values Pyramid** that enables you to identify the values that are most important to you at this point in your life. Knowing your values and prioritizing them in response to life's challenges opens access to living a life where your values are real and alive.

Part II expands the focus from the individual to members of a group, whether that be a family, a team, a business (or family business), or an organization of any kind. We explore what it means to have shared values within a group and how to have conversations with the group about values.

Three Resources for Completing Your Values Work

This book provides all of the information you need to define your personal and shared values and understand how to use them to shape your priorities and choices. We've found over the years, however, that many people desire visual and tactile tools to help them process information. We offer three pathways that help you do this work:

1. **The worksheets** inside this book. You can use the instructions in each Learning Journey to identify your values, understand why they are important to you, and work with others to identify and implement shared values.

2. **Our Values Edge Toolkit**. We discovered that people and groups benefit from having more concrete guidance, especially when working as part of a group, to develop shared values. For those reasons, we created our Values Edge Toolkit.

3. **Our Online Toolkit** provides a web-based space where you can sort, rank, and produce your own Values Pyramid for the first Learning Journey, as well as complete tasks in other Learning Journeys.

The Values Edge Toolkit

Our Values Edge Toolkit provides physical materials (such as a deck of values cards, stickers, display cards, and action plans) that advisors, coaches, and consultants can use to lead sessions for individuals, teams, families, and organizations. Having a physical deck of cards to sort your values is helpful and makes the Learning Journeys tactile and immediate. You can sort and re-sort the cards as you think through what is important to you (and re-use them throughout your life). These tools and sessions help increase purpose, engagement, resilience, and alignment, which support well-being, strong relationships of trust, and accountable performance. The toolkit includes a 110+ page facilitator's guide and worksheets for continued reference. Training is available for individuals and groups, as well as access to a learning community for additional resources and support.

The Values Edge 2.0 Toolkit is available at www.theValuesEdge.com.

Learning Through Action

This book offers more than just a few provocative ideas about values. The addition of Learning Journeys will lead you on a practical path toward using what you learn to look at your own values and make them real and operative in your life. If you read the chapters and then complete the activities, by the end of this book you will know how to:

- define and act on your own values.
- explore and deepen your personal values.
- understand others' values.
- generate guiding values/principles for a group, organization, or family.
- use your values to help you face challenges, make choices, and create policies and practices that align your values with your actions.

It's not simple to live a life based on values. Values are challenging and often difficult to live by. Crises, distractions, and pressures inevitably interfere. We can regard values as beacons, beckoning us toward the light, even when darkness and obstacles that need to be overcome emerge. We hope this book will help you define your beacons and live a life more in line with your aspirations.

PART I

~~~~

Identifying Your Values

CHAPTER 1

Finding Meaning Through Values

If we asked you what gives your life and work meaning, how would you answer? Most of us would respond, "our values." We believe our personal values form the core of our path to becoming good human beings. Values represent ideals we hold as "good" in themselves. They steer us toward selecting courses of action that will be congruent with them. That's why values are frequently called **virtues**—goals that we feel make us better people. Our character is shown by our values, which express deeply set moral principles.

Values bring order to patterns deeply embedded in our motivation and action. They develop from childhood as we imitate and learn from family, friends, teachers, and the media. They are a source of the meaning and drive that compose our lives. They lead to a deeper, more productive life.

Most people would like to live more by their values, but they often feel that their environment—opportunities they face, their station in life, other people, workplaces, and/or the community—makes it difficult. Overcoming those limitations takes time, effort, and creativity, involving difficult and risky choices, so it's not for the faint of heart. This is an active and ongoing process.

The chapters here in Part I will help you begin reflecting on and talking about your values with others. Here in Chapter 1, we'll explore the many facets of values and how they can help you live the life you want to live.

Values Reflect Your Identity

Values define who we are and what we stand for. They provide the foundation for behavior, motivation, career, and life choices that determine what we consider important and how we make decisions. They form a personal fingerprint to define us in a meaningful way.

Values are not discrete and independent islands operating independently. When linked together, they enable us to experience a coherent sense of who we are, what we do, and why we do those things. But we are more than a collection of values. Each person must find ways to link their values to what we call **personal identity**, formed by our words and actions. Many of our values are constants, beacons that guide us through our lives. Nobody lists eating, drinking, breathing, or sleeping as core values because we just do these things without conscious consideration. Values are about complex actions that are not obvious and automatic but require active choice to express.

Personal values emerge from our unique life experiences. When you act in accordance with a value, you feel good, satisfied that you have done well. We weave our personal values into the narrative story we tell ourselves and others about who we are. And when we live by these stated values, we are perceived by others as *authentic*. Values help us to chart a path for personal growth and move toward a life purpose. They offer a basis for decisions about how to pursue that purpose effectively.

Defining our values helps us understand and build our personal identity. Reflecting on how values are expressed by our actions gives us a way to measure how closely they match our values. This alignment results in feeling like our lives have a sense of coherence and personal authenticity.

One of the first researchers to define and categorize values and how they organize our behavior, Milton Rokeach, noted:

> Once a value is internalized it becomes, consciously or unconsciously, a standard or criterion for guiding action, for developing and maintaining attitudes toward relevant objects and situations, for justifying one's own and others' actions and attitudes, for morally judging self and others and for comparing oneself with others.[1]

What Is a Value?

A *value* is defined by Webster's Dictionary as a "principle, standard or quality considered inherently worthwhile or desirable."[2] The etymological root for "value" is *valor*, which means strength. Values are a source of strength, because they give us the power to understand our choices and more fully take action. Our core values are deeply held and tend to remain consistent throughout our lives. They form the direction and guidelines for day-to-day behavior. They help us organize our lives and stay on track during change and turbulence. Other values emerge when we encounter different realities and overcome challenges in different stages of life.

Psychologist Shalom Schwartz differentiates values from needs, preferences, or attributes:

> A value is a (1) belief (2) pertaining to desirable end states or modes of conduct, that (3) transcends specific situations, (4) guides selection or evaluation of behavior, people, and events, and (5) is ordered by importance relative to other values to form a system of value priorities.[3]

---

1   Milton Rokeach, "A Theory of Organization and Change Within Value-Attitude Systems," *Journal of Social Issues* 24, no. 1 (January 1968): 13–33. See also: Milton Rokeach, *The Nature of Human Values* (Free Press, 1973).

2   "Value Definition & Meaning." Merriam-Webster. Accessed July 14, 2025. https://www.merriam-webster.com/dictionary/value.

3   Shalom H. Schwartz, "Are There Universal Aspects in the Structure and Contents of Human Values?" *Journal of Social Issues* 50, no. 4 (Winter 1994): 19–45.

Schwartz notes six main features of values:[4]

1. They are beliefs linked to **emotion**; when activated they are infused with feeling.

2. They are desirable goals linked to action.

3. They transcend specific actions, choices, and attitudes to become **general principles** guiding action.

4. They serve as standards that **guide our choices** about what is good and bad, worth doing, and legitimate, even if they are not fully conscious.

5. They can be **prioritized** in order of importance.

6. There is a **trade-off** as our actions relate to multiple values.

As you can see from this description, values are multifaceted, representing emotions, actions, and guidelines. Let's explore how these attributes play out in our lives.

Properties of Personal Values

We all have a set of values, although it's common not to have a clear idea of what they are and how they work. Let's focus on five essential properties of values to frame the decisions you'll make later about which ones to focus on.

Values are aspirational; they motivate us to stretch and grow.

Personal values are *aspirational*, representing how we would *like* to act, even if we don't always achieve those ideals. Aspiring to values provides the bridge toward a more complete expression of them in your life. They inspire us to achieve virtues that form our character. Values are reinforced and informed by religious and

---

4   Shalom H. Schwartz, "An Overview of the Schwartz Theory of Basic Values," *Online Readings in Psychology and Culture* 2, no.1, (December, 2022), https://doi.org/10.9707/2307-0919.1116.

ethical codes, which provide further authority for core values we share with others. Specifying them as your personal values can inspire you to express them more directly as everyday hallmarks to guide your current choices and your future life.

Values are guidelines, not "shoulds."

We can mistakenly think of values as "shoulds" that tell us what we can and cannot do. But they are not meant to be rigid rules that constrain us. Rather, they serve as a source of energy, motivation, and inspiration that empowers us. When we care passionately about something—when we value it—we are propelled by strong internal energy to act on it. But they leave us space to act flexibly when situations call for difficult choices.

Values don't make decisions for us; they just justify and make our choices clear. If you feel something goes against your values, you'll face the choice of whether to speak up or maintain harmony with silence. We all get bombarded by requests to support different actions and groups. Values can help you decide whether to visibly support a cause or put it aside.

Values evolve with our lives.

Values differ from personality types, traits, competencies, or temperaments. They are not ingrained or inflexible. They evolve and are developed and enriched by new experiences. We alter or reconsider them by conscious choice when our circumstances change. Values reflect preferences and directions that, while not always conscious, can be sharpened or shifted to have more impact as our life changes. They are part of our learning process, as we strive to be better at expressing them.

As we learn and grow, meet life's challenges, and make everyday choices, we are influenced by our values. Each of us absorbs values from our upbringing, life experiences, parental behavior, family culture, and ethical/religious frameworks. We then combine them into a framework for making sense of our life and guiding our decisions and choices.

To adapt and flourish, we are always calibrating and modifying how we see the world. Values are not inherently within us. Nor do we simply absorb them from outside and then live them; rather, we "try them on." We adapt them to our current circumstances and either follow or reject them. As we grow and change, some of our values evolve and transform.

In other words, values adapt, shift, and evolve as we move through different stages of life. At one time, we might interpret "respect" as being totally focused on how an individual speaks to another, whereas at a different time it may be more defined by how an individual thinks through the impact of their actions on the larger ecosystem.

Our priorities or emphasis can also evolve. At any given time, some values are emerging while others become less important. And as a person achieves some life goals and abandons or reinterprets others, they begin to adopt some new goals and life choices that lead to emphasis on different values.

For example, some values you find important when you're in your early twenties will likely be different than those you focus on in your fifties or yet again in your eighties. A young person may not worry about health or physical self-care, instead spending time taking high risks, seeking adventure, or pursuing lofty professional goals. Into middle age the focus moves toward accepting who you are and what you have done, rather than radical change. By that time, our values will probably increasingly focus on maintaining daily health and possibly focus more on deepening relationships and family. A young single person has different values than a married person with three small children.

Further, how we express a value varies by circumstance. For example, how we exhibit a value of "self-expression" will be different in a professional or business environment than in a recreational one.

Values sometimes conflict.

We all adhere to multiple values in our personal, work, and community lives, which take us in different directions. In a complex environment, there will always be multiple experiences, beliefs, and values that can be important and possibly contradictory. This means facing some **values tensions**, conflicts where we struggle to balance our values. We may find that there is not enough time to act on all values, that acting on one value may interfere with actions for another, or that acting on a value may run counter to other commitments in work and life. Values are a continual consideration in an active life.

For example, parents are often presented with a particularly demanding child, and they want to please them. They also want peace and quiet. And they also want to be fair to their other children. They feel caught. Do they bend to the loudest voice and then try to make things right by doing something for the others, rather than stick with their original value?

Or consider a situation where you care about a close friend who has been there for you. Then this friend does something egregious that goes against your values around honesty, and you're tempted to cut ties with them. But your values around forgiveness and friendship call for a conversation. What do you do? Avoid or engage?

A third type of situation where we often see a tension between values can be seen by entrepreneurs who grew up in families with very different values about what success looks like. A woman named Ginny, for example, experienced limited resources when she was growing up and was taught to be conservative in her job choices and very careful with her finances. But she experienced repeated success in her risky entrepreneurial business ventures, and by her third venture was considered wildly successful.

At that point, she realized she had a newfound desire for a more low-key endeavor: one where she could move to a ranch to raise horses. This desire was brought on by a reemerging appreciation for values of peace and work/life balance that came from her family. She had a difficult time explaining this shift to her mom. Having built a life around a hard-earned career and financial success, her mom kept telling her to get a good job as a nurse! She experienced a tension between sticking to her value of carefulness and the hard-work ethic that had made her successful and seeking out that better work/life balance. The latter choice flew in the face of what her family (and even she!) had considered a worthwhile path.

These tensions are reasons we feel so strongly about making your values explicit. Doing so helps you anticipate and face these tensions directly and openly, and try to discover a creative way forward that combines them. (This is a theme we'll revisit throughout this book.)

Everyone's highest values are different.

Countless models organize types of values. They are usually displayed in one of two formats, either as a ladder or a circle (see Figure 1.1):

- In **ladder** models, values are arranged in a step-like hierarchy. The inference is that moving up the ladder represents "better" values (more important, essential, more deeply spiritual).
- The other form is a **circle** (or wheel), where values are arranged around a center point according to overall themes or styles.

Implied hierarchy (higher on the ladder is better)

No hierarchy. Each segment is connected to all other segments.

Figure 1.1: Comparing ladder and circle (wheel) models

Ladder-type models have several limitations, including the fact that, in our opinion, there are no best, superior, or higher values. Making a hierarchy of values can lead to conflicts between people that do not seem resolvable. For example, a value like "be healthy" is no more or less important than something like "practice open-mindedness" or "spirituality." They are just different.

Also, a ladder suggests that personal and moral development share a common pathway. That is, the way the values are arranged as steps on a ladder implies that a person's development of values follows a specific trajectory, representing a pre-defined progression of concerns, levels of interest, and attention to higher levels of human expression. Most human beings do not see themselves moving along such a well-laid-out path and, in fact, would most likely resist such a structured approach. Different moral codes, national identities, ethnic cultures, or lifestyles can create different paths of equal "value."

In contrast, circle- or wheel-based depictions of values focus on their inter-connectedness. They are designed around the notion that human beings espouse many values, all of which are important. Each person arranges their values around a unique common core, with a set of supporting values.

This approach feels more authentic to us. Society is built from blending many kinds of choices and situations. Wheel models affirm individual differences and how they harmonize and blend into organizations, families, and communities. No value is better than any other; all of them are valuable and useful to human life. Together, they express the richness of individual differences and human communities, and the multitude of paths people can take as their personal values evolve.

Another reason we prefer thinking about values in terms of a circle or a wheel rather than a ladder is that a circle has no specific start or ending point, no predefined sequence or progression. As we discussed, values shift in priority throughout our lives. But making a value a priority does not make it superior in any moral sense. Deciding something is a priority simply provides more guidance and clarity when you need to respond to your current circumstances.

We often experience this when someone faces a sudden or an unexpected health challenge. They might, for instance, reorient their values and behavior to focus on exercise, diet, and social engagement instead of the achievement-focused activities they had previously prioritized. Or they might do so when losing a job leads to a reevaluation of what success means and what lifestyle they want. As we discussed, values change in priority at different times. None of us lives by or practices all our values with equal emphasis all the time in perpetuity.

Making Your Values Matter

The Canadian philosopher and theologian Bernard Lonergan[5] suggested that your life is a work of art, and each person can be an artist creating his or her own life. How you live your life, make choices, and respond to your experiences stems from your values and life purpose. If you let your life just happen, you are being passive and not doing the work you can do to live a full life. You are not likely to be pleased with the results.

Values matter. A person who lives by values, or a family or organization based on values, can embody excellence. Such people and institutions are magnetic—they attract others because they seem deeply alive and are continually striving to embody their ideals. Their example offers a powerful alternative to a reactive existence, as their values base enables them to set and reach powerful goals; to have the courage to navigate change and sort through complexity; and to shape a long-lasting legacy.

Knowing your values and prioritizing them in response to life's challenges opens access to living a life where your values are real and alive. Throughout this book, we'll guide you through a discovery process that can be used alone or in groups to identify and clarify values and then connect them to your behaviors, actions, and achieving your highest goals. You'll see that there is no one set of values for success; everyone's values are unique and special.

Our underlying message is that having a clearer understanding of your values will make it easier to support better choices, build better relationships, and hone your performance. Values must be clearly articulated to be actionable, so let's get started with that work with Learning Journey #1.

---

5   Pierrot Lambert and Philip McShane, *Bernard Lonergan: His Life and Leading Ideas* (Axial Publishing, 2010).

Identifying Your Priority Values

The goal of this first Learning Journey is to identify the values most important to you as you face decisions and choices. This will help you focus, define, and organize your life and deepen your ability to realize your life's purpose and act upon it. You will start by selecting 15 personal values that are most important to you, then prioritize them into a Values Pyramid, an example of which is shown in Figure LJ1-01. See the caption for the interpretation.

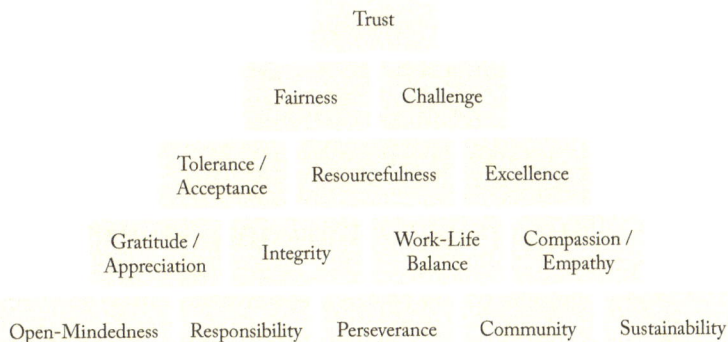

Trust

Fairness   Challenge

Tolerance /   Resourcefulness   Excellence
Acceptance

Gratitude /   Integrity   Work-Life   Compassion /
Appreciation   Balance   Empathy

Open-Mindedness   Responsibility   Perseverance   Community   Sustainability

Figure LJ1-01: This person started with a list of 64 values, identified the 15 that were most important to her, then arranged them in the pyramid. Her version indicates that responsibility is the value that matters most in her daily choices, decisions, and actions, followed closely by family and friends (the second tier).

CONTINUED ↓

The Values Pyramid you develop here will be used in later activities to help you look more deeply at the origin and nature of your values and define a future path to make your values a fuller and deeper part of your daily life.

Background for This Learning Journey

The first step toward harmonizing our actions with our intentions is to consciously define a set of values that help structure and organize our life choices. By defining these values, we narrow the gap between what we want to do and what we actually do.

But experience has shown us that identifying our values isn't as easy as it might sound. For many years, when we held leadership sessions, we'd ask people to name values that were important to them. People struggled to provide answers, and we were asked numerous times, "What is a value—can you give examples?"

We discovered through these sessions that the simplest way to help people clarify their values is to start with a prepopulated list of possible values and let them choose those they connect to. We could help them by providing a comprehensive but curated list. So we started collecting examples from our work and formulated a list of values to provide the starting point for conversations. After many revisions, we settled on a list of 64 values that represent the vast universe of values identified in our working sessions. That list forms the foundation of this Learning Journey.

Step 1: Identify values that are important to you.

The table provided here lists the 64 values we identified during our decades of work with individuals and groups. As you read through the list, think back over the past several months and place a checkmark next to those values you view as guiding your actions, choices, and behaviors over that period.

❑ Achievement

❑ Ambition

❑ Appearance

❑ Autonomy

❑ Beauty

❑ Belonging

❑ Challenge

❑ Collaboration

❑ Communication/Openness

❑ Community

❑ Compassion/Empathy

❑ Competence

❑ Confidence

❑ Consistency

❑ Courage

❑ Creativity

❑ Curiosity

❑ Enthusiasm

❑ Excellence

❑ Fairness

❑ Family

❑ Flexibility

❑ Forgiveness

❑ Friendship

❑ Fun/Play

❑ Gratitude/Appreciation

❑ Harmony/Resolving Conflict

❑ Health

❑ Helpfulness

❑ Honesty/Candor

❑ Humility

❑ Integrity

❑ Intimacy

❑ Justice

❑ Kindness

❑ Learning/Personal Growth

❑ Loyalty

❑ Mentoring

❑ Moderation/Frugality

❑ Nature

❑ Open-Mindedness

❑ Optimism

❑ Peace

❑ Perseverance

❑ Power

❑ Prosperity

❑ Purpose

❑ Recognition

❑ Relaxation

❑ Resilience

❑ Resourcefulness

❑ Respectfulness

❑ Responsibility

❑ Risk

❑ Security

❑ Self-Control/Discipline

❑ Self-Reflection

❑ Spirituality/Faith

❑ Stability

❑ Sustainability

❑ Tolerance/Acceptance

❑ Tradition

❑ Trust

❑ Work/Life Balance

Notes on using the list of values:

- If the last few months have not been usual in your life due to vacation, big challenges, illness, life events, etc., think of a recent period when your life was more like it usually is to guide your sorting. We acknowledge that the values you select may be different now than they were at other times in your life, but this activity is focused on the here and now.

- There are no right or wrong choices about the values that are important to you. This activity is just a starting point for helping you explore how your choices, behaviors, and actions represent different priorities so you can understand yourself and others better.

- Some of the values are paired with similar ones. You should select them if one of the pair seems to fit and not get confused if you see them differently. Think of the pairs as either/or.

- It is common to realize that all these values are important, and we may agree with them, but force yourself NOT to check them all. Do this selection quickly without getting stuck in overanalysis. Acknowledge that at different times in your life your selection would be different. Right now, you are looking at a snapshot of the actual values that figure into a fixed time in your life.

- If you struggle with whether to check a particular value, try to think of a specific example of how that value has manifested in a recent choice, decision, tension, or conflict. If you can't think of a specific example of an action or choice guided by that value, do not check that value.

Step 2: Select your top 15 values.

Obviously, 64 values are too many for any individual to commit to. So, we'd like you to review our list and identify 15 that you most closely identify with. A reason to identify only 15 values is that it is very hard to remember and actively apply more than 15 values, very difficult to keep a long list of values actively guiding your life at any one time. Prioritizing into a shorter list will help you make sense of your most common behavior.

Count the number of values you have checked. If you have more than 15, go back and reduce the number to the 15 you most actively live by. If you have fewer, add some other important values that didn't make your original list until you reach 15. Enter them in the following table or anywhere you are keeping track of your work.

MY MOST IMPORTANT 15 CURRENT VALUES

1.	2.	3.
4.	5.	6.
7.	8.	9.
10.	11.	12.
13.	14.	15.

Step 3: Arrange the 15 values into a pyramid.

Now, prioritize your values in order of how important they are in making decisions and choices in your daily life. Organize them in the following pyramid. Start with the value that is most central to your life as reflected in your behavior and place that value at the top of your pyramid. Continue to place your values into the pyramid in descending order of importance. You may work through several arrangements to come up with your pyramid.

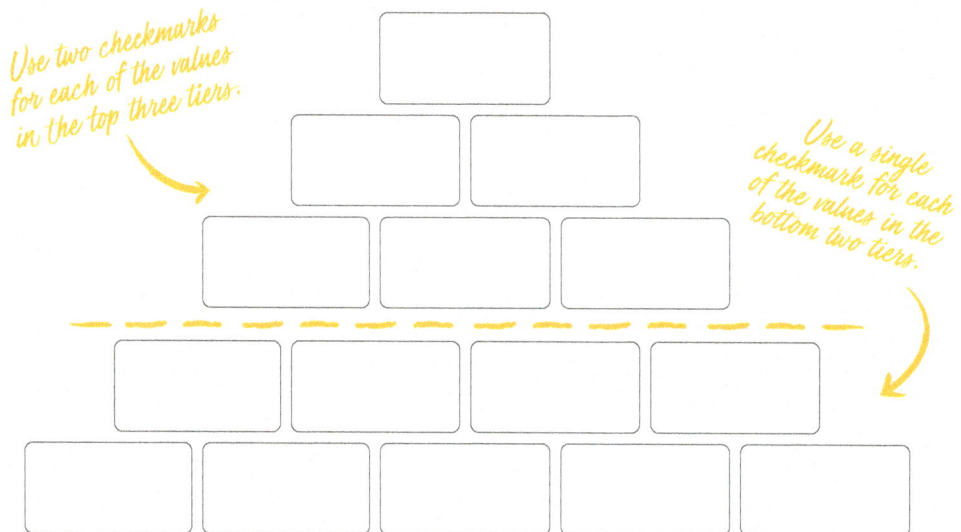

Use two checkmarks for each of the values in the top three tiers.

Use a single checkmark for each of the values in the bottom two tiers.

Now that you have sorted, ranked, and created your Values Pyramid, you have the foundation for taking your values into action. The next chapter will help you understand how to connect your values to decisions, choices, and everyday actions.

CHAPTER 2

Understanding the Relationships Between Values (the Values Wheel)

Working with individuals and groups to clarify their values, we noticed that people saw their values connecting together in common themes, concerns, life goals, or moral principles. The patterns formed by relationships between common values are what we call your **Values Drivers**.

This chapter presents our model for understanding the relationships between values. We discuss the concept of Values Drivers in depth. Then in Learning Journey #2, you'll have the opportunity to define your own drivers.

Identifying Clusters of Related Values

If someone tells you they value collaboration, fairness, and communication, can you see a connecting thread? We do. We see these as fitting into an overall theme of relationships between people. They are focused on how you interact and engage with other people and respect their integrity.

This example illustrates that values exist in related groups. We use the term **cluster** to reflect sets of values that share a theme or principle. Clusters provide a framework that makes it easier for people to tell a story about the values they've applied throughout their lives. Clusters also enable people to see how their own values link to common elements of their style and direction. For example, having several values in one cluster indicates the importance of that theme to that person's life.

Since values are complex, multifaceted, and often ambiguous, placing them in clusters is not an exact science. There is overlap, and values take on different meanings in different circumstances (life stages, environments, challenges).

To identify clusters within our model, we began with the list of 64 values you sorted in Learning Journey #1. We looked for common themes that connected values and ended up identifying 8 clusters, reflecting eight different ways that people orient to their environment and make choices about time, tasks, and using their energy.

To further support our value clusters, we drew on the work of American social psychologist Milton Rokeach, who first divided values into two categories based on how they shaped your internal approach versus how you interact with others and with society. We modified his model and selected the following two categories:

- **Inward values** focus on personal motivations and directions a person navigates from. Some of these relate to temperaments and personality traits, but we believe that they are more properly defined as values because they can be modified and represent actions and paths that are chosen, rather than determined for you.

- **Outward values** focus on how you connect yourself to the external world, form relationships with others, and reinforce and support what you strive for. They are like the intrinsic values of Rokeach as they pertain to looking outside oneself into the end goals one wants to see and create in the world.

For each of these two broad groups of values, we defined four clusters that are similar in their focus, shown in Table 2.A.

TABLE 2.A: THE 8 CLUSTERS OF VALUES

Inward Clusters *Organizing Your Behavior*	Outward Clusters *Organizing Your World*
1. Mastery 2. Empowerment 3. Self-Expression 4. Well-Being	5. Humanity 6. Legacy 7. Relationship 8. Interconnectedness

You can find a detailed list of which values fall into which clusters in the next Learning Journey.

After sorting our clusters into these two categories, we built a visual depiction we call the **Values Wheel** (Figure 2.1), which arranges all eight clusters in a circle. (You'll note that the word "purpose" sits in the center of the wheel, and we'll get to that in a later chapter. For now, focus on the eight clusters.) The upper half of the wheel represents the four clusters of outward values (dealing with people and the world around you), and the lower half represents the four inward value clusters (those concerning your personal motivation).

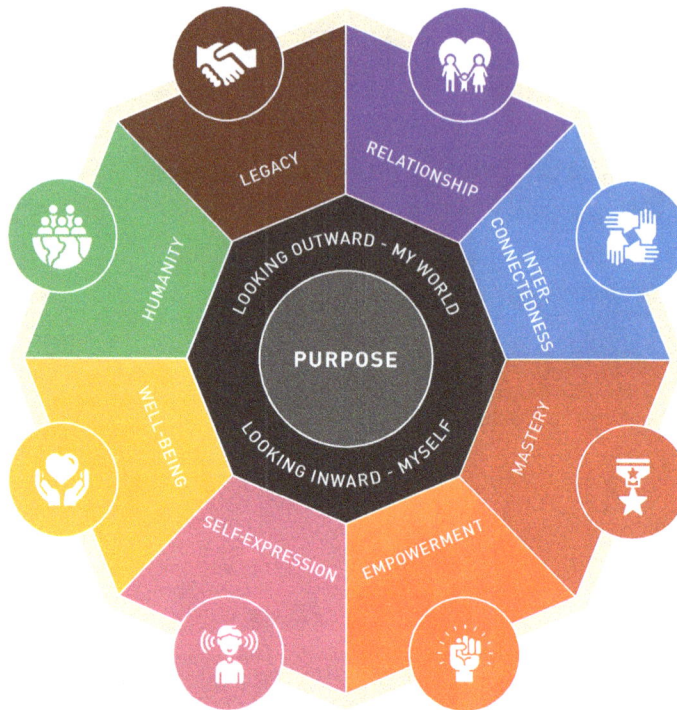

Figure 2.1: The Values Wheel

Take note of the color coding in the wheel.

Some years ago, we and other professionals who work with values realized that we needed to do more to help people understand the relationships
between values and provide visual aids to help people sort and prioritize their
own values. For that reason, we developed specific color coding tagged to
each of the eight clusters of values, and we carry the color coding into all of
the ancillary worksheets and products that our clients use when completing
a values exercise. For example, if you are working with our Value Cards that
can be found in our Values Edge 2.0 Toolkit, you'll see that each of the 64
cards (one for each value) is color-coded by the cluster it belongs to.

Identifying a Values Driver

Your Values Drivers are determined by the cluster theme that embraces the most values from your pyramid. In fact, people often have one or two major Values Drivers—one or two of the eight values clusters that contain several of their values. For example, in a pyramid of 15 values, suppose you have 4 values that lie within the *Self-Expression* cluster and 3 lie in the *Relationship* cluster. So, you might consider *Self-Expression* to be your major personal Values Driver and *Relationship* to be your secondary Values Driver.

Knowing your Values Drivers will make it easier to talk about your values and use them for making decisions and spotting areas of potential growth. It helps you link several values into a common pattern that describes you. In discussions, people can share and compare not just their individual values but talk about how their Values Drivers are similar or different. For example, a family may find several people prefer the *Relationship* cluster while others prefer the *Legacy* one. Adherents to each style can talk about how their values link to these styles and what each driver means in their choices and preferences.

Using the Values Wheel Model

The Values Wheel provides a framework that can be used by individuals to help them clarify their personal values and by groups (teams, families) to talk about shared values. It helps people with different individual values see how their values are part of larger clusters and therefore connected to values others may hold. These larger values clusters in the wheel can be used to organize multiple values into useful patterns to aid in talking with others about differences and commonalities.

And remember: Like values, none of these clusters are better or worse than the others; they are just different. They *can increase or decrease in importance based on challenges and circumstances.*

Identifying Your Values Drivers

Now that you have filled in your Personal Values Pyramid, you can explore how your values fit in with the 8 clusters in the Values Wheel and identify the pattern of inward and outward values that differentiates your Values Drivers.

Step 1: Which of your priority values are inward focused?

The first list included here lists all the values in the four inward-focused clusters, which connect values that determine how you express yourself in the world. Look at the values in your pyramid and place a checkmark in the list next to any inward-focused values listed in your pyramid. Note the name of the cluster(s) where you are making checkmarks.

Worksheet: Inner Values of Self-Motivation

MASTERY: Seeking advancement, success, standing out, dominance, and acknowledgment

- ☐ Achievement
- ☐ Ambition
- ☐ Competence
- ☐ Confidence
- ☐ Excellence
- ☐ Perseverance
- ☐ Power
- ☐ Recognition

EMPOWERMENT: Building capability, capacity, and commitment to self-direction for reaching your goals

- ☐ Autonomy
- ☐ Courage
- ☐ Open-Mindedness
- ☐ Optimism
- ☐ Purpose
- ☐ Resilience
- ☐ Self-Control/Discipline
- ☐ Self-Reflection

SELF-EXPRESSION: Fostering a unique life purpose by expressing new possibilities, innovation, and creativity

- ☐ Challenge
- ☐ Creativity
- ☐ Curiosity
- ☐ Enthusiasm
- ☐ Flexibility
- ☐ Learning/Personal Growth
- ☐ Resourcefulness
- ☐ Risk-Taking

WELL-BEING: Living a fun, well-balanced, vital life beyond work

- ☐ Appearance
- ☐ Friendship
- ☐ Fun/Play
- ☐ Health
- ☐ Intimacy
- ☐ Prosperity
- ☐ Relaxation
- ☐ Work/Life Balance

Step 2: Which of your values are outward focused?

Repeat the aforementioned process, this time for outward-focused values. This next list includes values in the four outward-focused clusters, which have to do with how you relate to other people and operate out in the world. Again, look at each value in your pyramid and put a checkmark next to any outward-focused values. Note the name of the cluster(s) where you are making checkmarks.

Worksheet: Outer Focus, Social, and Relationship Values

HUMANITY: Attention and energy advancing life in a meaningful global community

- ☐ Beauty
- ☐ Community
- ☐ Family
- ☐ Integrity
- ☐ Justice
- ☐ Nature
- ☐ Peace
- ☐ Sustainability

LEGACY: Continuity and respect for supporting and preserving accumulated wisdom

- ☐ Consistency
- ☐ Loyalty
- ☐ Moderation/Frugality
- ☐ Respectfulness
- ☐ Responsibility
- ☐ Security
- ☐ Stability
- ☐ Tradition

RELATIONSHIP: Living and working productively and comfortably with other people

- ☐ Belonging
- ☐ Collaboration
- ☐ Communication/Openness
- ☐ Compassion/Empathy
- ☐ Fairness
- ☐ Helpfulness
- ☐ Honesty/Candor
- ☐ Mentoring

CONTINUED ▶

INTERCONNECTEDNESS: Experiencing the unity, preciousness, value, and inter-relatedness of all living beings

- ☐ Forgiveness
- ☐ Gratitude/Appreciation
- ☐ Harmony/Resolving Conflict
- ☐ Humility

- ☐ Kindness
- ☐ Spirituality/Faith
- ☐ Tolerance/Acceptance
- ☐ Trust

Step 3: Identify your Values Drivers.

Your Values Drivers refer to the value clusters that represent your predominant values, those you use most often or to make your most important decisions.

Determine which cluster(s) represent the highest number of your values.

Start with an image of the Values Wheel that has several open circles in each cluster (see Figure LJ2-01).

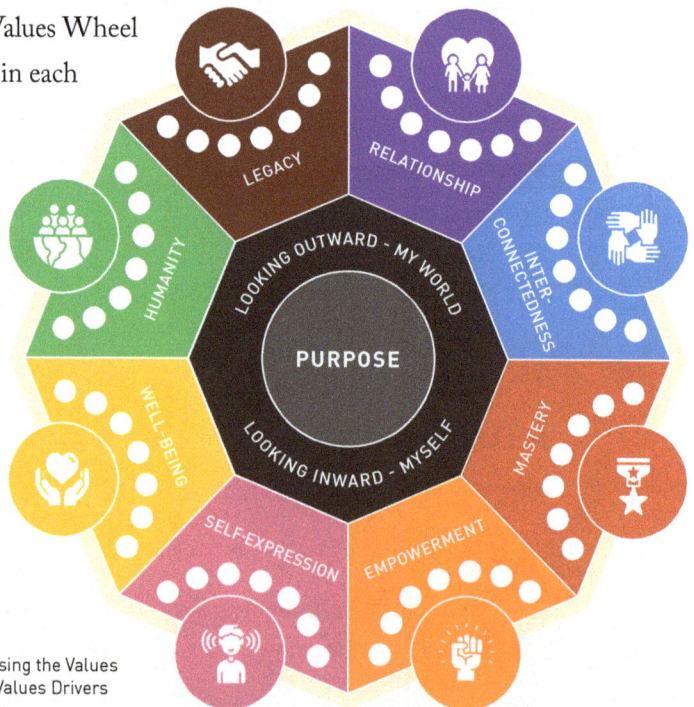

Figure LJ2-01: Using the Values Wheel to identify Values Drivers

For each value in your pyramid, darken one or two of the circles in the cluster that value belongs to. Darken two circles if that value is contained in the top three rows of your pyramid, indicating that that value is especially important to you. If the value is in the bottom two rows of your pyramid, darken only one circle in the relevant cluster (see Figure LJ2-02). That will give you a weighted indicator for each of the eight values clusters, meaning your highest priority values are more strongly represented in the outcome.

Figure LJ2-02: Using a weighted voting system to determine Values Drivers

For example, based on the priority pyramid used in Learning Journey #1, Figure LJ2-03 shows the result using the two-point system for the highest priority values.

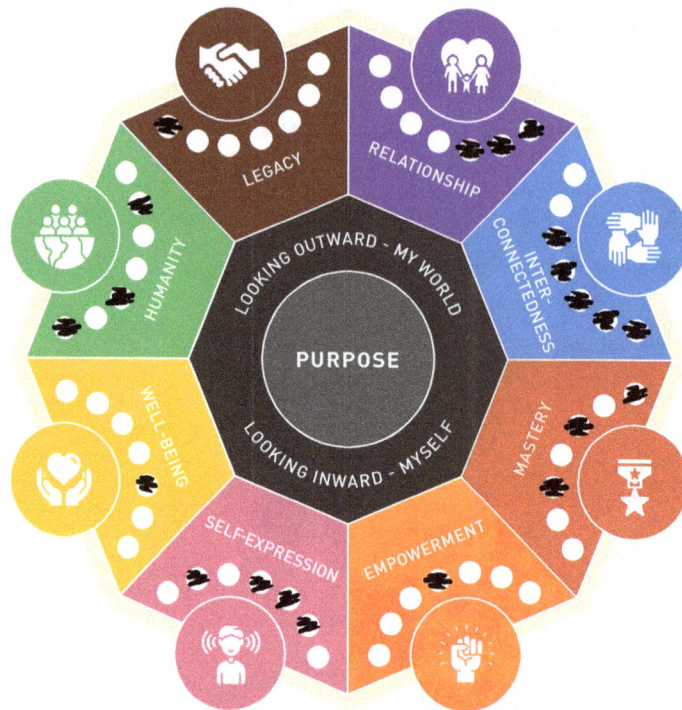

Figure LJ2-03: Weighted voting example

Interpreting the Results

The cluster with the most darkened circles represents your **primary Values Driver**. The cluster with the second-most values is your **secondary Values Driver**. Enter that information in the diagram. For example, if you have selected five *self-expression* values (one value in the top six and three in the bottom nine) and four *relationship* values (one value in the top six and two in the bottom nine), you can consider your primary Values Driver is *self-expression* and your secondary driver is *relationship*.

Most often, the primary and secondary drivers will include one cluster in the inward and one in the outward clusters; but there are sometimes exceptions. Either way, the two major drivers are a good indicator of the common focus. People can find common ground when they share a primary or secondary driver.

But if you are not comfortable and feel that another cluster is more characteristic of you, you can use that one.

Because this is a self-sorting exercise, feel free to make some judgments in identifying your primary and secondary drivers.

Exploring the Origins of Your Values

Your Values Pyramid tells you what your most important values are at this point in time. But why did you select those 15 priority values for your pyramid? Where do your values come from? They develop through your life experience and personal learning and decisions. In this Learning Journey you will reflect on major developmental experiences and transition points in your life and how your values emerged from those experiences. By looking back at their origins, you can become clearer about what each value means to you, how it is part of your life, and how to express it with more conscious intention in the future.

How Values Are Formed

Before diving into the reflection activities, let's take a quick look at how values develop. As is illustrated in Figure LJ3-01, they emerge over your lifetime, but primarily early in your life, influenced by your exposure to and interaction with multiple people and environments.

1		2		3		4
Culture Ancestors Parents Caregivers	→	Influence from Peers Social Role Models Heroes	→	Navigating Tensions Self- Authoring Choosing and Shifting	→	Harvesting Legacy Wisdom

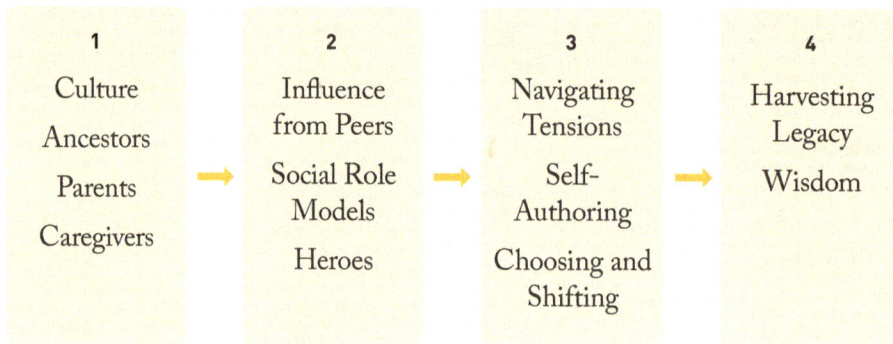

Figure LJ3-01: Stages of values development

1. **Culture, Ancestors, Parents, Caregivers.** You pick up your values first from your parents and other caregivers, and from the cultural surroundings of your early life and your religious traditions.

2. **Influence from Peers, Social Role Models, Heroes.** We pick up further values as we encounter inspirational teachers, media, friends, or groups. Their example moves and excites us to emulate them, to make choices that open new paths for our lives. Their behavior connects to values we are moved to follow and embody.

3. **Navigating Tensions, Self-Authoring, Choosing and Shifting.** As we've discussed, while values are relatively stable over the course of our lives, they are not static. As you grow outside of the culture of your birth and encounter values from other cultures, you may be drawn to new inspirations, tensions, and challenges. This requires you to reflect, choose, and shift as you create your own unique values. You begin to have agency and control over your values.

4. **Harvesting Legacy, Wisdom.** As we mature, we have time to consolidate and reassess experiences and harvest some core values that have endured throughout our lives—sorting out what values we have cherished and used to guide us in enlivening our lives and our work.

Now it's your turn to think through these stages of values development.

Reflection Activity #1: Exploring Culture — Ancestors, Parents, Caregivers

Parents are our first and deepest value influencers. They usher us into their values systems, which also reflect religious or spiritual traditions. Parents want their children to develop strong values, usually those they themselves hold, and strive to make that happen.

Parents, teachers, caregivers, and religious institutions are invested in passing on and perpetuating their values; they play an important role in upholding cultures and identities. Young children are impressionable and open, and parents, teachers, and spiritual leaders are on the front lines of values training. They exert influence with rewards, slogans, symbols, and rules to create a social order in which people can live and work cooperatively. As we grow, our world becomes more complex and diverse, and we are exposed to more voices promoting "desirable" values.

Parents often approach early values learning with the notion that their words are enough—if they repeat/teach a value, it will be transferred. But along with those words, young children see how their parents behave. As has been observed, "Values are caught, not taught." Young people learn more deeply by example and observation than by exhortation. We "catch" our values from our parents/caregivers/family, etc. Sometimes, maybe too often, the words and the actions do not match. Actions are more immediate and concrete and more influential than words. Children quickly learn that there is a difference between espoused and acted-upon values. They usually adhere more strongly to the actual than the espoused ones.

Parents are the first and often most powerful teachers, engaging their children and initially compelling them to adhere to rules of proper behavior that become values. Young people see how their parents talk about others and how they treat them, and they learn how to fit into their culture. These lessons are deep and powerful. They can be positive and inspiring, comfortable and nurturing, or, in sad cases, destructive and painful. These early lessons have a huge influence on our lives, but in today's fluid and complex environments, it is common for young adults to engage in exploring, accepting, rejecting, or modifying these early-life lessons as part of building their own values framework.

Many families have a family identity connected to a multigenerational tradition and culture. This stems from their ethnic and religious beliefs, and it is taught early to children. Values work often begins by defining the legacy family values and asking which ones should be kept and adhered to, and which ones need to be modified and redefined. Your own values reflect and build upon family traditions. As you begin to define your values, people and families often begin with their legacy values and traditions. You then see how your personal values reflect or modify these traditions and inquire as to why and how they have changed.

Exploration Questions

- Consider each of your parents. What values did each of them stand for?

  _____

  _____

- How have these values infused your current values?

  _____

  _____

- What values have you absorbed from other key relatives/caregivers?

  _____

  _____

- How have these values infused your current values?

  _____

  _____

- What values emerged from your family culture?

  _____

  _____

- What are some of the traditions and rituals that came from your ancestors/culture?

  _____

  _____

Reflection Activity #2: Exploring Peers, Social Role Models, Heroes

Young people learn from the example of those around them and from the mentoring and teaching of key people in their lives (teachers, helpers, relatives, clergy, coaches, friends' parents). They often have a teacher or even a famous person whose example shines for them and leads them to hold certain values. Various forms of media provide heroes and role models that deeply touch youngsters. They are exposed to many people who they may respect or admire (leaders, role models, sports figures, celebrities, etc.). Helping them identify what behaviors they admire can help them connect those behaviors to values that they wish to follow. Engaging in social conversations about what teens and young adults admire provides a way for them to curate their values.

Values are also shaped by life events—challenges, triumphs, and failures, which provide lessons in what values are needed to avoid or overcome unnecessary damage. Values are shaped by every major experience in our lives. Each one provides a thread in the tapestry of your values. Values do not make a neat one-and-done package that fits seamlessly together, but rather evolve over time.

When you complete a phase of your life (e.g., marriage, birth of children, new jobs, active parenting, retirement, leadership role, succession) pause and see this transition as an opportunity to refresh, reaffirm, or realign your values. For example, as we enter school, we begin to be influenced by role models outside of our families. Friendships, media, sports, and other activities expose us to people who affect us emotionally and provide inspiration; and sometimes hard lessons about values misalignment.

Exploration Questions

Recall a special hero, teacher, relative, or friend who deeply moved or impressed you.

- Who was that person, and what excited or inspired you about them?

_____

_____

CONTINUED ▶

- What did you admire and want to emulate about them?

  _____

  _____

- What did you want to learn or embody from them?

  _____

  _____

- How did you use the lessons you learned? How have those values continued to influence your life?

  _____

  _____

Reflection Activity #3: Navigating Tensions— Self-Authoring, Choosing, and Shifting

By the time we are adults, we have been saturated with experiences, relationships, and choices that interact, conflict, or lead us down different paths. As we mature, we sometimes participate in religious, community, leadership, or educational programs that explore and affirm certain values. They offer space to sort through and reflect on our values to ensure they align with the life we are currently living. People's values are linked to their personal identity. This identity is both internal, in that it offers us a sense of who we are, and external, in that it helps determine the way others see us. We want as much as possible for our internal sense of identity to match how we are seen by others. Living with a conscious set of values gives you a yardstick to assess your choices in difficult situations and subsequently change course or look for a new path that allows your values to prevail.

People develop or change their values when faced with crises and setbacks that deeply affect them. For example, a personal tragedy or an event that seemed important at the time, such as rejection from a social group, career disappointment, failure to win a competition, loss of a job, or loss of a friendship, can lead you to question your values.

We make sense of our lives by making choices that align with our changing values. As we navigate life events and challenges, we try out, reject, and reformulate our life purpose. Life does not happen to us; we react, we forge a path, and we take risks and exhibit courage and determination. Encountering predictable transitions and challenges can provide a deeper sense of coherence and meaning to the values we develop.

These challenges can also lead us into internal crises. Having doubt and concern about the meaning of your life and work can emerge from feeling burned out or disheartened about the focus or composition of your life. These more existential crises can also spark renewal and a shift in values. Spiritual leaders such as Mother Teresa have written about facing a crisis of faith, during which a person's core values come into question. These can also occur in response to key transitions: divorce, marriage, critical illness, and life trauma. These times prompt deep questioning about what we value, possibly leading to new choices and different decisions.

In developing their values, every person can share a story or a life lesson that arose from adversity or a challenge. We face a challenge and act, then we create a narrative that encapsulates what we learned and took away from the crisis. These narratives help us make sense of how these experiences have shifted our focus, choices, and life view.

Exploration Questions

- What challenges, setbacks, and crises have shaped your life?

  _____

  _____

- What clusters would increase your sense of resilience, if you put more attention toward them?

  _____

  _____

CONTINUED →

- What cluster could leave you more vulnerable, if you do not attend to it?

  _____

  _____

- How might these patterns influence the choices and decisions you make in the future?

  _____

  _____

- How did these experiences help you rethink what you do and what you want in life?

  _____

  _____

- What shifts have these tensions created in your life?

  _____

  _____

- How have you modified, reconsidered, or shifted your values in response to these experiences?

  _____

  _____

Reflection Activity #4: Legacy— Harvesting Wisdom for the Next Generation

As you navigate a life filled with influences, challenges, and turning points, you will have many opportunities to reassess and refocus what is important in your life. Gathering the wisdom of your insight and experience is an important gift to share with those who will follow you. Taking time to review what you have learned and communicate it to the next generation provides a sense of continuity to those who follow you. With increased experience and perspective, people often gather up their insights and lessons with the intent of passing on wisdom to the next generation. They tell stories to their children to share who they are. They become mentors—guides to help them on their own paths.

Gathering such experiences is a form of life review that combines your life experiences, beliefs, and hopes for the future. Sharing your wisdom in conversations, letters, or poems can honor what you have experienced and create a bridge to those who will want to understand what mattered to you in the future. Share your hopes for the future—what do you hope for in their lives? This gathering and sharing can provide a tangible way for others to understand what mattered about your values and your life.

Exploration Questions

- What are some events that have had the greatest impact on your life? How have they contributed to shaping your values and beliefs?

  _____

  _____

- When things got tough, where did you find comfort?

  _____

  _____

- What were some of your most valued traditions?

  _____

  _____

- What have you been most grateful for?

  _____

  _____

- What are some of the enduring values that have continued to enliven and support you throughout your life?

  _____

  _____

CONTINUED

- What are some values you would like to pass on?

  _____

  _____

- What are some of the patterns you are proud of?

  _____

  _____

CHAPTER 3

Aligning Behavior and Values

L iving by your values is not a single decision but a work in progress. To be more resilient and adaptable, you need to not just have values but also actively draw on them in making major life choices. Even though values clearly complicate your life and challenge you to do more, they ultimately lead to a deeper, more meaningful, and productive life.

Once they have created a Values Pyramid, many people feel they are done. But having a list of values, even if organized in a pyramid, doesn't do much for you in terms of making them enter your life. A value is not real if it is only an intention—it is real only when it is *lived*. And if you try to live by a set of values, you may find that actions that support one interfere with others. Moving from a values list to a values life represents a challenging journey.

To make that transition from ideals to reality, you need to express each value through your actions and actively develop the degree to which you live your values. That's what we'll talk about in this chapter, which is followed by a Learning Journey where you identify ways to make your values come alive.

Seeking Congruence and Alignment of Values

Many people do not consciously consider the role and use of their values, leaving them unexamined as guides to decisions and actions. Yet whether they are conscious or not, we have seen that values drive our behavior. Because they may not be everyday topics of discussion, we can forget to pay attention to them to inform choices and decisions, and instead live an unconscious or entirely reactive, passive life.

In fact, we may *assume* that our values are automatically applied in our lives. But upon further reflection, we see that our values are often vague, unclear, and contradictory—and not applied consistently. It's easy to consider ourselves virtuous because we *feel* that we're doing good in our lives, especially if we don't look very deeply at whether what we are doing fits our values.

This is a problem because when values are neglected or ignored, we can feel disconnected from our basic existence, leaving us without energy and passion. Ultimately, this neglect of inner alignment can leave you feeling empty and adrift, even depressed. We have labeled this alienation, a malady that can shadow and diminish our lives.

In contrast, when you align your values and your actions, you become more engaged, effective, and motivated in your own path, enhancing your example and leadership to enrich your work, family, and organization. If you get out of balance with living your values, you can change your behavior. Clarity about personal values, purpose, and mission provides guidance in the following areas:

- deciding how to allocate your time, money, and resources.
- deciding among career paths to pursue.
- making hard choices in the face of pressure.
- acting in accordance with a strong set of spiritual guidance.
- engaging in long-term causes.
- being willing to work long hours for a community initiative or a political candidate.

We ponder the questions in each of these areas as we seek to build a meaningful life that contains well-being, fulfilling work, and strong and positive family relationships—a life that makes a difference. People who live close to their values have an internal fuel that powers them. They actively seek and discover new opportunities and relationships that align with those values. As a result, when values are manifested in our lives, we feel whole and fulfilled, with a deep sense of purpose and goals to strive for.

When we fall short of living our values, we can course-correct and change our behavior. In fact, we continually face the challenge of aligning our behavior to fit our values and often fall short of who we want to be. The desire to make our values fit who we are speaks to the aspirational property of values we discussed earlier, motivating us to learn, change, and grow.

Having a clearer understanding of your values will make it easier to support better choices. People with greater resilience in the face of challenges have a deeper understanding of their basic values and use them as guidance, helping them to understand "why" they are taking the actions they are taking and finding the motivation to do better.

As management psychologist Chris Argyris describes in his books,[6] he would confront people when they acted in ways that did not agree with their values. For example, he recounts one instance when he pointed out to a leader that they talked about collaboration but tended to lecture their team members rather than ask them about their ideas. Argyris stresses that people have to work hard to make sure that their behavior corresponds with their values. He strongly suggests that they get feedback from others about whether they are living by their values. Argyris uses the term *congruence* to describe the alignment between values and behaviors; we and others use the term *authenticity*.

---

6   There are many books by Argyris, but a good place to start is *Knowledge for Action* (Jossey-Bass, 1993), which outlines his theory of action learning and his concepts of congruence and authenticity.

> ### Congruence leads to resilience.
>
> Being able to form a coherent narrative of what is happening in your life is a core capability to creating resilience. Values are a source of strength because they help you discover a clear path to act in complex, ambiguous situations. In fact, one of the core aspects of people who respond to challenges in a resilient way is that they have the ability to make sense of their life experiences in relation to the values they hold. Using your values to reaffirm what is important to you supports an enduring sense of continuity and purpose in your work and your life.

Authenticity is sometimes referred to as "walking the talk"—acting in a way that aligns with what you say you are going to do. One of the most common requests employees have of leaders is that they be authentic and transparent: telling the truth, even if it is upsetting. A person acting authentically is more impactful and comes across with more authority. Part of behaving authentically is having the ability to connect your values to a clear expression. Values help make sense of your life; they provide a foundation for how your actions fit together.

Argyris stressed the need for—and the difficulty of—being consistent between our values and our actions. We become authentic or congruent when what we want, what we believe, what we say, and what we do all come together. The desire to make our values fit who we are leads us to embrace the aspirational property of values we discussed earlier, motivating us to learn, change, and grow.

Closing the gap between values we aspire to and our current behavior is an ongoing adjustment. While some of us feel that we make good choices and our values and lives are in harmony, others fret and struggle to achieve this harmony and integration. We can feel pulled in different ways and struggle to do what we want to do. What happens when we fall short? How do we recover or reconnect with the vital thread of purpose? What do we do when challenged by those around us that our actions are not authentic—that they are misaligned with our values?

Using Misalignments to Prompt Change

Everyone has had a moment when they sensed that a particular job, friend, or venture is not quite right. But how many of us take the time to reflect upon the warning and reconsider? Many people simply go along with things until a moment comes when they wake up and see that their life is not the life that they want to live.

Learn to pay attention to signals that either affirm that your values are aligned with your choices and actions or that a choice may run counter to your values, such as the following:

- We sense that something we are about to do is not the right choice.
- We know a task or project is important to us because it's the right thing to do.
- We face adversity and struggle to achieve long-term challenging goals.
- We decide to do something to help or support another person.
- We choose to undertake a specific project, a job, or a direction over many others.
- We opt to work with somebody, connect to a social or political group, or develop a personal relationship.

The more we reflect about challenges like these, the more natural it becomes to question and change them as we try to achieve our goals in life. We all face adversity, disappointment, setbacks, and tragedy in some form or another. These events challenge our values and provide opportunities to affirm them. Remembering values that have brought you through these disruptions reminds you of what can be gained from falling out of alignment and recovering balance.

There will always be times when your behavior/actions do not align with your values. Imagine you are having the following experiences:

- You are at a meeting and get called out for saying or doing something that the others feel is wrong. Your values are under attack. Do you attack back, shrink away, apologize, and placate the critics, or stand your ground? How can your values guide you to better pursue your intentions?

- Someone brings to your attention how your actions do not seem to be matching your values. For example, maybe you say you value listening and respect for others, but then someone points out you tend to dominate conversations or continually interrupt others. How do you acknowledge this slippage? Do you apologize? Do you ask for help?

- You feel inspired by a community volunteer opportunity and at the same time you have other commitments and are fully engaged. Do you walk away or follow the calling to see what the new possibility offers? What values does this activity represent that you may have been not giving enough attention to?

- A job opportunity tempts you with its attractiveness and benefits. But you experience a discomfort, due to a tension you can anticipate that could challenge one of your important values. How do you express the tension you feel in a way that helps you stay in alignment with your values?

- You are asked to do something by someone you care about, or your boss, and you feel that this action is wrong, unethical, and misaligned with your values. You feel pressure and fear that if you don't go along you will suffer. Do you give in? Or do you raise a challenge, voice your objections, or even refuse to go along?

- You are about to start a new relationship and find yourself hesitating, sensing that something is a bit off. Will you heed this signal and explore this concern in a way that does not foreclose your opportunity for a relationship? Or just move forward and hope for the best?

- You look at what you are doing and ask, "Is this all there is to life?" How can you use your sense of your values to look at what you might have been ignoring to deepen your focus for the future?

- You are looking at two divergent choices that lie before you. Both have benefits and outcomes that would enhance your life. How can you bring your values into the exploration of these two paths?

What choices do you make in these situations? How do you act? It's not always clear. And if you are under pressure or stress, it can be especially challenging to adhere to your values. This can lead to a situation where you ignore your values and take what seems like a more necessary and practical path. This is a common way that values are eroded or set aside. If you feel that stress or pressure leads you to ignore a value, you might at least consider that path and then ask when or if you can reaffirm living by a value. Looking at stressful events in relation to your values is an important task.

Making Your Values Visible

Making a value visible offers an opportunity to build motivation to make a difficult choice rather than taking the easy path. As we've seen, every person faces adversity, disappointment, setbacks, and tragedy, and these situations can lead us to ignore or disown our values. Living in a way that conflicts with what you believe can be a source of depression and drain the energy of active commitment and satisfaction from what you do. Conversely, inspirational stories of heroism in the face of adversity offer models for values-based living that we can learn from.

The process of identifying and articulating the behaviors/thoughts that best express your values can potentially reveal a gap between what you think is a way to fully manifest a value and how you currently act. It is common to aspire to a more inspiring expression of the values you selected. This clarity creates a personal core sense of coherence and alignment with how your values support your beliefs and actions.

People often avoid this clarification because recognizing that there's a gap between an aspired value and your actual behavior is uncomfortable. This is especially apparent when a peer, friend, or family member points out such a gap. But this can lead to an opportunity for a conversation that allows both people to explore the differences in their views of the values in question so they can understand the different interpretations of what behaviors indicate those values to each person. This exploration and resetting is especially important in relationships that endure over time in the workplace or family. It is very common for two people to think they understand what the other means by a value and end up in a misunderstanding, which can lead to disappointment or a falling out. If they avoid the issue, they can become estranged.

> **Identifying values is not a one-time event.**
>
> In light of all the factors we've discussed thus far, it's clear that our lives are dynamic—and our values must be dynamic too. Identifying and clarifying our values is therefore not a one-time event, but a continuous process of reflection and adjusted action. This process helps us get more aligned and in tune with our values and to build a shared values community around us.

The Wisdom of Values

Living by values is a process of moving toward a life built upon clarity, courage, and conviction, linked to a specific purpose or major life goals. Having clarity about your values will help you make tough choices about the life you want to lead. You may also decide to change or remove yourself from certain activities and settings that do not allow you to live by your values.

Over time, we become clearer about what we believe and more capable of aligning our goals with our actions. We then do things that allow us to live more deeply and act with intention. When we experience this deep connection between our values and our actions, this is what we call **wisdom**. A wise person is clear about their life purpose and lives by it. As we mature, we aspire to be seen as wise and to have a respected place in our community. Staying true to our values fosters deeper connections with our family, friends, and colleagues and helps us articulate how we contribute to our workplace and community.

Values are difficult to live up to. If it were easy, we wouldn't have to refresh our commitment and attention to our values. But we regularly face situations where our values are challenged. Fairness, for example, is a common value, but what does it mean for a parent or a leader who sees one person as more talented or valuable than the other? The meaning of being fair is a source of great stress in work and family.

> To hold a value is not a passive activity but an active set of choices and a path that we must choose, often with difficulty.

We encourage you to make your values an explicit part of your life. People who live close to their values have an internal fuel that powers them. They actively seek and discover new opportunities and relationships that align with those values. As a result, when values are manifested in our lives, we feel whole and fulfilled, with a deep sense of purpose and direction.

Defining, exploring, and taking a critical view of how we can align our behavior with our values serves an important purpose in a chaotic world. When we face difficult choices, we can engage our personal foundation to allow us to choose what we want according to our values. That is what is offered by the path we propose. To hold a value is not a passive activity but an active set of choices and a path that we must choose, often with difficulty.

Living Your Values

This Learning Journey explores the behaviors you use to express your values. This Journey will explore how you and those around you—family, friends, coworkers, and community members—see you as authentically expressing your values. These activities will sharpen your ability to express your own values, describe your values to others, and be part of conversations where values are applied to choices and challenges.

As you undertake these activities you become more aligned and connected to your core values. Only when you act on your values directly can you know and feel you are living according to them. As we will see, this alignment is important as you connect your values with those of your family and your workplace.

The exercises up to this point have been ones you can do by yourself, but now we suggest that you start involving others in your explorations. Doing so will help you broaden your learning by sharing your values and their expression with people who are important to you. This opens you to different perspectives, allowing you to gain deeper insight into how you are living (or not living) your values.

Reflection Activity #1: Becoming Accountable for Acting in Alignment with Your Values

Values without action show intent but do not behaviorally demonstrate how you live/embody your values. By making your values explicit and concrete, you deepen your understanding of them and are better able to express them to others. This strengthens your ability to connect your values to your actions and demonstrate personal accountability.

Every core value contains aspirational areas that can become fuller expressions of that value. It is helpful to identify that *stretch*. By imagining an outcome, you can energize yourself to take on more challenging actions; by seeing yourself in your mind's eye, you make it more likely that you will try that action. In this activity, you envision specific actions that reflect and honor each of your core values.

- In the first column, list the 15 values in the order you have placed them in your pyramid.

- In the second column, consider some of the obstacles and sources of pressure that make it difficult to live by that value.

- Then, in the third column, for each value write specific behaviors, actions, processes, etc. that represent how you demonstrate that value. This is not easy and will take time. You may also want to use more space to write these actions down. You might make a checkmark next to the actions that you have taken recently that embody that value.

- In the final column, note how you aspire to demonstrate that value, ways you might express that value in the future.

Value	Obstacles	Behavior/Action/Process	Highest Expression/Aspiration
#1			
#2			
#3			
#4			
#5			
#6			
#7			
#8			
#9			
#10			
#11			
#12			
#13			
#14			
#15			

Keeping your values at the center of your focus requires diligent attention. It is easy to become focused on daily actions and not see the deeper pattern of how your values can guide your choices. Taking time to link your actions/behaviors to your values gives you a sense of focused coherence. The larger values clusters can be a way of consolidating and connecting your actions to your core values.

Reflection Activity #2: Creating Stories That Exemplify Living Your Values

A value is much more than a single word. So, when you consider your Values Pyramid, you can make each value clearer by defining what you mean by each value and how you practice it. You should consider details such as:

- what exactly it means to hold a certain value.

- what happens when you act in concordance with that value.

- what having that value looks like.

- what behaviors/actions support that value.

A powerful way to capture these details is to tell a story of how you practice your central values, perhaps even recalling a time when you found it difficult to live up to that value. Such stories bring life to your values and link them to the important things you do in your life.

For example, if you identified *collaboration* as one of your core values, reflect on how you engaged others in your last project. Did you pull in diverse opinions about the metrics to use to assess your project? Did you reach out to others who may not have initially been interested to create a path for their engagement? How did you demonstrate interest/openness to ideas that were different from your own?

Prompts for Developing Stories About Your Values

- What are some of the experiences that have led me to develop my values?

- Who are some of the important people who helped me shape my values?

- How did these values become important in my life?

- How have they changed over time?

- What has stayed the same?

- How do these values manifest themselves in my life now?

- How might I want to express these values in the future?

Reflection Activity #3: Sharing Your Values with Others in Your Life

Another effective way to deepen your understanding of, and strengthen your connection with, your values is to talk with people important to you about what your values mean. Those people can potentially challenge you and help you look more deeply at what your values mean in action. And they can tell you when you are out of alignment.

This kind of discussion not only helps you sort out your own thinking, but is essential for creating aligned teams, relationships, and communities. In fact, families, work groups, and organizations often take time to clarify their values together. When they face a lack of alignment and find clarity, they strengthen their commitment and connection to each other.

Discussing values in a group is easier if everyone involved has created their own Values Pyramid; then you can all share and compare values and what they mean. Such a conversation can lead to clarity and alignment of values, and a deeper understanding of what each of you stands for.

Discussion between yourself and others is critical because even if people identify the same value as being important to them, that doesn't mean they have the same interpretation of its meaning. Because we all have different life experiences, people have starkly different takes on what a value means. For example, fairness is a value that can have many different expressions.

- What behaviors reflect fairness between parents and children, spouses, and employer and employee?
- What changes if a person also holds the value of equality and links it to their value of fairness?

As people share these kinds of details and tell stories, take the time to listen and explore how other people define their own values; you can then share yours and talk with the others about the areas where you differ and where you agree. This discussion yields the most meaning and connection when you enter it with a sense of curiosity and openness to hearing about the values of the other person in the conversation. Discuss the differences and see if there is any path to common ground.

After sharing stories, you can expand the discussion by finding commonalities and areas where people express something unique and special. This can lead a team or a group to see the richness of the diverse values each person brings. As we will see, this lays the foundation for further discussion about what can emerge as shared group values.

Getting the most benefit from your individual values clarification happens when you can talk with others to appreciate their values and find areas of synergy and complementary interest. This involves adding detail to the one-word values in your pyramid and identifying actions, behaviors, or choices that you think reflect your alignment with that value.

Exploration Questions

- What is one value that you turn to most often?
- What would someone who knows you say you are doing to support this value?
- What past action shows your support for that value?
- How would you express your alignment with this value in making decisions?
- How would you describe your definition of this value?

Reflection Activity #4: Acknowledging Emerging Values

The values in your pyramid are current active values, a snapshot of your most recent life choices. As we've discussed, because your life does change, there are often circumstances, relationships, or challenges that can open possibilities for new values to emerge. Your pyramid contains some important enduring values as well as some that may be less enduring.

There are values you did not select for your current values that you would like to bring more fully into your life. These are our **emerging or aspirational values**. These may represent new interests or areas that you have not had time to develop or new life lessons from increased maturity. They may support areas of life or work that are beginning, based on where you are in your life cycle. These emerging values might provide needed balance or indicate a refocused attention as changes occur in your life (parenthood, retirement, marriage, etc.). Making explicit and paying attention to these emerging/aspirational values provides opportunities for growth and change.

Select one or several values that were not on your pyramid of 15 that you want to deepen or experience more fully. Return to the original list of values that were not in your pyramid and consider what other values you might like to bring into your life as you grow and develop. What new behaviors/actions might bring that value into your life?

For example, you might select *friendship* and then focus on inviting someone you like to spend time with you. Or maybe you want to practice greater sustainability by reducing your household waste or eating more vegetables. Selecting aspiring values is a way to grow and develop as new stages of life emerge.

Reflection Questions

- How do your emerging values represent a shift in your current focus?
- What kinds of behaviors/actions would represent your emerging values?
- Where are these values already starting to bubble up?
- How will you make room for your new behaviors/values?
- What will take on less importance?

CHAPTER 4

Creating Purpose Through Values

B eing able to make sense of your life and express to yourself and others why you do what you do refers to what we call your **life purpose**. Purpose has been called "true north," the direction and goal of your life journey. It can be seen as a guiding force that shapes your actions, decisions, and the overall arc of your life. People attain significance and respect by organizing their behavior toward a goal expressed as a life purpose.

Individual purpose can be thought of as an enduring, overarching sense of what matters in a person's life. People experience purposefulness when striving toward something significant and meaningful to them. Having a clear purpose that you can state to yourself, and to others, helps you lead a resilient life. Having a coherent sense of what your life is about provides an anchor to assess your actions and align them more fully with your ideals.

You will have noticed that *purpose* sits in the center of the **Values Wheel** model introduced in Chapter 2, indicating that we view it as the central focus of a values-based life.

Your purpose becomes a foundation for making choices, following your direction, and navigating through complexity and change. It provides an overall theme that unites all your values into making a life that matters. As your life changes, different values become important and therefore your purpose may be focused differently. Purpose serves as an internal compass rather than a rigid goal. It deepens as you navigate changing circumstances. Purpose gives you a shorthand for decision-making and taking action in specific areas of life and work.

Your life purpose is not a fixed target but an evolving direction that gains depth and clarity by holding a focus on your core values. This chapter explores how to distill your purpose from your most important values so you can strengthen alignment between your values and choices. Then you can capture these in a written **Purpose Statement**. You might want a Purpose Statement for your family and personal life, and another for your work life. This, in turn, helps you make difficult decisions and share with others who you are, what you believe, and what you consider important in life.

Multiple Paths to Discovering Life Purpose

Purpose is not a predefined blueprint you can copy from anyone else, even a wise teacher or spiritual leader, but an evolving framework shaped by your life's experiences. It is open to continuous refinement while having a deeper fixed essence.

Many scholars and philosophers have written about how a person can become attuned to this deeper purpose. They argue that rather than experiencing life as unfocused and random, a person benefits and becomes more complete when they discover and live by such a path. We will not attempt to review that wisdom here, but rather offer some thoughts about connecting purpose to one's defined and aspired values.

How do you uncover your life purpose? The paths to achieve this are many and often convoluted!

For some people, purpose emerges seemingly naturally as an expression of the choices, actions, and interests in their lives. It gets clearer and clearer as they focus their attention on things that they find satisfaction and engagement with. This focus builds more opportunities to engage with activities, study, and work that express this direction until it is clear that all these actions, choices, and opportunities form an overarching reason or purpose for their life.

These lucky people are aware of their purpose early in life. They are in touch with a central focus for what most matters to them and direct their lives according to this inner direction. As their life unfolds, they modify, deepen, and fill out this vision. They are aware from childhood that they are "called" to become an artist, entrepreneur, naturalist, journalist, actor, teacher, or carpenter. This clarity offers a deep sense of identity and shows a path to expressing and developing it. Now the challenge is to choose how best to realize and embody that path.

Other people build their life purpose through a trait, talent, or strength. For example, someone who is known for being a joker, problem-solver, or dependable friend could turn that trait into a career (e.g., comedian, manager, or life coach). Some of these people come to their purpose later in life, when they have fewer obligations and pressures. Reconnecting with an earlier whisper of a purpose when someone is older can consolidate many life experiences into focus. When this happens, many choices that had seemed separate and disconnected are now seen as connected. It can be a mid-life financial windfall or success that draws your attention, gives you satisfaction, and begins to lay a path toward a territory in which your purpose manifests.

Some people have a harder time connecting to a life purpose. They flounder, find it hard to choose, or can't seem to get in touch with how to connect their values. In this search, they seek mentors, elders, role models, and projects that seem to have a spark of what they value. Having clarity about your values can help you begin this journey of exploration.

Many people get caught up with finding their one true purpose and stumble for fear of getting it wrong. Others step into a role expected by their family or people around them without taking the time to question how that fits with their values. The limitation of being given a "purpose" by others can result in a mismatch, leading such people to feeling empty or lost and needing to rediscover what really compels them.

Some people have a sense of what their purpose is and might use the "fake it till they make it" approach to explore areas of activity that match their interests.

Discovering Your Own Purpose

Our advice? Give yourself time to explore your values-based direction and allow your purpose time to manifest itself. The top values in your Values Pyramid are a great starting point for articulating your purpose.

But keep in mind that your purpose will likely evolve from investing time and energy into meaningful endeavors that over time connect to a deeper pattern of focus and meaning. One cannot simply select a purpose, but can hone in on one by participating in activities, making decisions, and seeking out experiences that may then reflect a pattern of meaning. You can craft your purpose by continuously reflecting on how your actions and values are reflected in your purpose. Living with purpose requires continual evaluation and realignment, considering changing circumstances and one's evolving values.

Also, we must point out that in a single life you will take up numerous roles that are manifested in many circumstances, and it may be daunting to be limited to only one purpose. It might help to think of purpose as not a single point but a directional pursuit of a cluster of core values that help you achieve greater meaning and impact. Therefore, purpose is not a single value but rather a synthesis of all the values that we stand for. And vice versa, your personal values form a path to making your purpose come alive. Values help you reflect and continually check in with how you are acting in alignment with your purpose.

Writing a Personal Purpose Statement

One way to more fully express your values is to craft a **Personal Purpose Statement**, which can express the outcome/impact that your values support. It provides a structure for gathering your personal values. A Purpose Statement offers an integrated summary of the goal and direction your personal values are intended to support. It can also function as your "elevator speech," where you quickly tell another person what you are about, beyond your job title.

A Personal Purpose Statement is distilled from how both your inward and outward Values Drivers influence your choices and actions; it provides a shorthand summary of the intent of the desired impact of your values in action. It functions as a quick reminder as you take actions, make choices, and renew yourself. It is most potent when it is a short statement, no more than a paragraph, that articulates the reason/meaning for your life.

A Purpose Statement answers three questions:

1. What you are doing in your life?

2. How are you doing that—what specific activities are at the core of this?

3. Why is this important—what values does it fulfill?

You can use your Personal Purpose Statement to sort through values tensions where more than one value seems important. It provides a way to act with a sense of satisfaction and even fulfillment in becoming the person you want to be. It helps you communicate what is important to you so that others can connect with you.

We'll walk you through the steps for crafting a Personal Purpose Statement in the next Learning Journey.

Purpose and Meaning

The universe does not provide you with a life purpose. To design your life and live it, you must name, embrace, and commit to a life purpose. Purpose is a choice rather than an inherent trait. You deepen your purpose by choosing activities that express this personal identity, which can function like a personal brand.

For an individual, purpose is not a singular goal; it is an overarching direction that provides a framework for making sense of multiple jobs, careers, decisions, and actions over the span of your life. For families and organizations, there can be multiple purposes to connect social, economic, and leadership standards for their product, brand, employees, and community.

Defining your purpose provides a structure for making meaning out of life's experiences. When you make it explicit, you have a beacon to guide you as you encounter life's experiences. You can use it to communicate the overall reason that guides your choices and what gives you a deeper sense of meaning. This is different from short-lived experiences of meaning. It serves as a continuous thread that connects separate life experiences into a narrative of meaning that can bring life to even seemingly mundane tasks.

For example, fulfilling the purpose of raising children is filled with many tasks, such as cooking, cleaning, and nurturing a safe and loving environment for growth, etc. These tasks become fulfilling because they are linked to the larger purpose of raising the next generation of strong citizens. All these tasks take on meaning when they are linked to a larger purpose.

You can't have meaning every minute—circumstances change and affect your ability to live your purpose. You will have times when you experience a disconnected feeling. Going back to your purpose or values, as a "meaning repair kit," can get you back on the path.

Living with the Gap Between Purpose and Action

You will not be able to live a purpose-filled life all the time. There will be times when circumstances intervene, and meaning/purpose will seem to have gone away. These times of confusion, doubt, or pain are signals to return to meaning-making activities, however small, to rekindle your sense of purpose and meaning.

Purpose is not a plan but a direction to continually explore and try out new pursuits. It takes vigilance and courage not to engage in pursuits, relationships, and ideas that no longer align with your current values. Living on purpose requires a commitment to continuously refine your purpose to align with shifting values and circumstances. Engaging in regular self-reflection helps you reconnect your purpose with your values.

A purpose-driven life is less about discovering a single ultimate direction and more about continuously aligning actions with values to create meaning. Core values serve as the foundation for purpose, providing a resilient framework for decision-making and personal fulfillment. By actively investing in meaningful experiences and adapting to evolving values, individuals can cultivate a lasting sense of purpose that enriches their lives and leadership.

Through intentional reflection and action, purpose remains a dynamic and guiding force, shaping both individual fulfillment and broader organizational impact.

Practical Strategies for Strengthening Purpose with Values

This Learning Journey will help you clarify and refresh your purpose as it evolves over time. You will most likely return to this set of questions time and time again as you adjust and refine your purpose to be in sync with changing circumstances in your life. You may recalibrate your purpose based on encountering new experiences and insights throughout your life. This requires curiosity, self-reflection, and a willingness to acknowledge the gap/tension between your aspired purpose and your actions.

This Learning Journey leads you through the steps for drafting a Personal Purpose Statement and then shows how you build a stronger connection to that purpose by reviewing your daily actions.

Step 1: Explore your top values.

To begin, look at the top 3 (or maybe 6) values in your pyramid, and consider what clusters they represent. In the following worksheet:

1. Compare your Values Pyramid to the Values Drivers you discovered in Learning Journey #2. Then list your top 4 **values clusters**—those that represent the most values—in Column 1 of the table, sorted by where they appear in your Pyramid. Put number one closest to the top and go down from there.

2. In Column 2, note the behaviors/actions that you are taking that support that cluster.

3. In Column 3, summarize the impact of these actions. For the sake of what are you doing these actions?

4. In Column 4, imagine some additional actions that you might take to more fully express that value in the future.

5. Summarize the impact that these actions might create.

1 Top values clusters	2 Actions you are doing that currently support/ express these values?	3 For the sake of what impact are you taking these actions?	4 Future actions that might support these values?
Example: harmony/ resolving conflict	Mediation, teaching, counseling kids	World peace	Supporting a political candidate dedicated to education
1.			
2.			
3.			
4.			

Step 2: Draft a Personal Values Statement inspired by the values.

Now try creating a Personal Values Statement summarizing how your values support a bigger impact and a long-term path for your life.

_____

_____

_____

_____

Here are some examples of Personal Purpose Statements:

- Preserve and share history, inspiring future generations by supporting Native American museums.

- Foster sustainable business practices to protect our planet for future generations.

- We want to increase the health of all the communities we are part of and inspire our children to follow this path.

- Promote financial literacy to help all family members make informed financial decisions to build our financial and non-financial wealth for generations to come.

- Create innovative products that improve the lives of people in the world by exposing them to beauty and a life that touches everyone.

- Create musical performances that bring joy and inspiration to people.

- Advocate for the rights and well-being of children around the world.

Considerations for Writing a Purpose Statement

While there are no binding rules for writing a Personal Purpose Statement, there are some suggestions to consider.

- Avoid naming a single outcome. For example, "I intend to write great novels and strive to get them published" can become a terrible weight. It holds you to a single purpose that may never be fulfilled, and it limits you by closing doors to other options.

- Be open to alternative expressions of your purpose. There may be other ways to express the values you wish to express, ways that might more clearly define the experience you want to create. When you know why you want to pursue a goal, you are open to other paths that might take you toward it. For example, a person who wants to be a great writer can find meaning and purpose in becoming a communications consultant for a cause they find compelling.

- Be willing to move beyond an early life purpose. You may find it can become a trap that holds you in a false pursuit of some direction that you are no longer engaged with, keeping you from fresh exploration and alignment with what really matters to you.

- Avoid oversimplification. Avoid naming a specific way of being, so you can be present and stay open to whatever life offers. Naming a way of being ("happiness" or "calmness") as your life's purpose creates passivity toward life. "I intend to live 'authentically' or 'ethically'" sounds nice, but how would people understand the impact of doing that?

- Don't give up before you really have tried something. One of the great regrets some people have is when they had a sense of something that might be meaningful, but that required learning, skill development, experience, and perseverance. They let their focus fade because it was not immediately within their grasp and went on to something else. Consider fulfilling a mission with a long skill development path.

Optional: Writing a Leadership Purpose Statement

Those of you in a leadership position may also find it helpful to write a **Leadership Purpose Statement** that concisely describes how your values support the impact you want to have as a leader. You can use this statement to communicate the vision of what you want the team/organization/family to achieve.

Think of a Leadership Purpose Statement as a summary of how your values will help you bring about an inspiring outcome or create positive impact for your team, organization, community, family, etc. That is, how will those entities benefit from your leadership? How does your work as a leader connect to these outcomes/results?

Leadership Purpose Statement Examples:

- I lead a specialist team aiming to create the right technological infrastructure to bring our many development programs into a web of smooth paths for our customers.

- My commitment to building a sustainable procurement process relies on supporting teams feeling successful and satisfied in bringing their best innovation and expertise to every customer challenge.

- I am committed to impact technology by innovating solutions for the common good.

- My leadership purpose is to seek out change that will spark innovation, creating a dynamic and agile organization that supports us to thrive in an ever-evolving landscape.

- I value teamwork and collaboration, and my leadership purpose is to foster a supportive and inclusive environment where everyone can contribute their best.

Strengthening Your Connection to Purpose with Daily Activities

You can use your daily activities that provide a sense of fulfillment to inventory your purpose. How do these activities create shared meaning for you? How do your values align with your actions?

- Take a moment to identify a small task/action, one that may reoccur in your life. Enter it into Column 1 in the table.
- Indicate your feelings about that activity in Column 2.
- Then explore how it is connected to a value that you hold as important in Column 3.
- Finally, write down how this chain of small actions connects to your larger purpose.

Daily activity	Feelings/Meaning your experience from doing this?	What value does this support?	Implications for my purpose
Example: washing dishes	Sense of completion, moment of joy	Beauty in my physical surroundings	Bringing sense of support for my family
1.			
2.			
3.			

You can strengthen your purpose by creating structured routines or taking part in values-driven activities. Commit to community service, beach cleanups, social support, etc. Using your values as an anchor can make the connection between what could be experienced as mundane activities and meaningful, purpose-affirming actions.

PART II

Using Shared Values to Create Resilient Families and Organizations

The purpose of this book is not just to illuminate the importance of personal values, but to demonstrate how groups of any type or size—families, teams, businesses, organizations, communities—can use values to build and sustain a thriving culture. The following chapters guide you in exploring the values that make up the shared culture of your family and your workplaces. Doing so will help you create clear and aligned cultures among diverse groups.

Here is a quick preview of what's to come:

Chapter 5: Shared Values = Shared Culture discusses fundamental concepts about shared values that are important for all groups to understand.

Chapters 6 and 7 and Learning Journey #6 are devoted to identifying shared values in families. This work can benefit any family, but is especially important for families that run a business together. It can help them clarify the differences between which values are shared by family members as opposed to values that will be used to run the business.

While we focus our presentation on business families, the process of creating a multigenerational shared family culture applies to any family, no matter what its level of financial wealth may be. True wealth is a quality—not a number—that can be part of any family.

Chapters 8 to 11 and Learning Journey #7 focus on identifying and implementing shared values for a business.

CHAPTER 5

Shared Values = Shared Culture

Values are not just for individuals; they are also the foundation for society and cultures. Individuals have values that make up their identity; when they become part of families, work, and community organizations, they become part of a shared culture that is made up of values that members of the group share.

Cultures share values that express their shared humanity and broader collective aspirations. Values have always been a part of civilization, forming the way groups of people perform collective functions like raising a family or creating a business, and how they respect each other's individual choices, work cooperatively, and live together for the common good. They represent the ways that people agree to treat each other and to join in activities to achieve a purpose greater than that which individuals can achieve on their own.

Shared values form the basis for community cohesion, the culture that defines a family, a work team, and even an organization's central focus. Families, social groups, and organizations define who they are, what they stand for, and what moral and ethical codes they endorse by the values they embrace. In that way, shared values create alignment and connection between group members.

People tend to judge others and be uncomfortable with groups driven by different values. Such distance is counterproductive today, where we must acknowledge and have relationships with diverse people and groups. Doing this is the human factor that determines our ability to live, work, and thrive as a species.

Setting shared values, purpose, and mission creates a foundation for what any group or organization is about. If you are inspired by a group's values, you are motivated to become or remain part of the group. If this is missing, people will find other things to do and other places to direct their energy. They will withdraw. Being explicit about shared values, mission, and purpose can catalyze the energy of a family, team, or organization. People will be more likely to take initiative; the organization will release creativity and innovation and be better able to make decisions that support a shared direction.

In short, finding shared values for a family, team, or organization generates a sense of inspiration, coherence, and resilience. It's not surprising then that groups seeking alignment have come to us asking that we help them identify, deepen, or refresh their shared values.

A Challenging Task

It is much easier to be comfortable in an environment where values are shared and unchallenged. But that is becoming less and less likely in our interconnected, global environment, where we face challenges we never expected. We are always bumping into people with different values. Further, as families or groups expand or evolve and members leave or join, values become open to review and adjustment.

Creating and maintaining group alignment and commitment is challenging in a society like ours, where different religious and moral traditions coexist in schools, civic institutions, communities, and workplaces, and can come into conflict. Individuals can either isolate themselves in a niche where they feel safe and comfortable or actively experience the tension inherent in facing the multiple perspectives different traditions offer.

Today, we can no longer rely on living within a single, consistent culture. Digesting and synthesizing multiple sets of values into coherent, useful, navigational principles is the ongoing work of individuals, organizations, and families. Such active engagement to discover areas of agreement across competing values systems cannot be ignored. The people within a group cannot just "agree to disagree" because there are policies to be made, practices to decide, and purposes to pursue—all of which will be less effective and enduring without the guiding hand of *shared* values at the core. More and more, people want to co-create their culture, not just accept what is offered, not blindly follow the construction of a single leader.

The ability to curate a blended set of shared values that allows all group members to align their choices is what differentiates a strong, thriving community from one where conflict or confusion may derail progress. Clarity is key: just as an individual should be able to explain their personal values and what they do to support those values, the same is true for families and other groups. The end goal of identifying shared values is making sure everyone knows what the values mean and how to apply them to daily choices.

Example of Shared Values

To give you a sense of where we're headed, here is an example of a culture and Values Statement from a family-owned business. Arnold Enterprises (a pseudonym) manufactures furniture to serve different markets with well-made, nicely designed furniture at affordable prices. They are facing cost pressure and difficulty finding good craftsmen and may need to modify their business model.
Here is their Values Statement:

> Our culture seeks to inspire and empower our people to innovate and develop bold ideas that will help Arnold Enterprises achieve lasting impact. Our culture, and the core values that support it, should create an environment that spurs our team to think outside the box, feel comfortable

pushing the boundaries of what is possible, and signal confidence in our team's ability to make change happen through our philanthropic efforts.

Here are some examples of the values that make up Arnold Enterprises' work culture:

- We are adaptable and comfortable with ambiguity.
- We are intellectually curious, open-minded, objective, humble, collegial, and receptive to feedback.
- We are action-oriented with strong self-direction and self-motivation skills with the ability to work simultaneously on multiple projects.
- We are able to interact confidently and collaboratively with team members and navigate relationships with external experts, government leaders, advocates, and individuals.

Arnold Enterprises' values reflect who we are as an organization, help us accelerate our strategic goals, strengthen our resolve, anchor us to our mission, and guide our decision-making. Our leaders will demonstrate the following core values that inspire the Arnold Enterprises team to make a difference.

- Respect for Ourselves & Others
- Audacious Action
- Collaborative Engagement
- Depth of Thought
- Clear Communication

Preview of the Shared Values Process

How does a family or work group develop such shared values? We always begin with the clarification of each individual's personal values. This lays the foundation for developing a Values Pyramid and a Personal Purpose Statement, as described in Part I.

After the individual's values have been clarified, the group can move to distilling shared group values, leading to a set of principles and/or a statement of shared purpose and mission that can guide the group in their day-to-day decision-making and actions.

Having a Values Statement and set of principles provides a family or company with an anchor as they clarify how well the values help them fulfill their mission and purpose. Having a public values credo—either within the family or within the community—sets an intention to uphold a set of values and to be publicly accountable for them.

Developing these principles involves ongoing conversations that include reflection, analysis, and reformulation to fit the current conditions and challenges of an organization or family. These conversations work best in an environment where there is respect and confidentiality, so differences can be candidly explored and acknowledged. We will outline roadmaps for navigating this process for families (Chapters 6 and 7, Learning Journey #6) and for teams and businesses (Chapters 8 and 9, Learning Journey #7).

> **Values identification is not one-and-done.**
>
> The identification of shared values is not a one-and-done undertaking, but a process of renewal and reengagement as a family or group moves through challenges, generational change, and governance recalibration.

Making Shared Family Values Real, Not Ornamental

With great expectations and enthusiasm, many groups identify their shared values and write a Values Statement. But too often, the glow fades when there is no path to move those values into action.

Living up to values is not easy. For example, what happens when, upon closer inspection, two team members realize they have divergent views of what a particular value means and how it should be demonstrated? Or when a company that has pledged to value its people and remain in its community finds that changing market or economic conditions would make it advantageous for it to move jobs to another community?

For values to serve as a useful resource for decision-making, the group needs to identify behaviors/actions that demonstrate these values and incorporate them into the policies and practices of the family or business.

Values are strongest when groups or families are not just happy to have a Values Statement posted on a wall, but actually hold each other accountable for how the values are applied to key policies, processes, and decisions. They do this in the following ways:

- They set time for conversations about what the values mean.
- They develop policies, practices, and working relationships aligned with their values.
- They use a Values Statement to make it clear what the organization or business offers an individual.

Values come alive when they are reinforced by stories that support how they have made an impact on a group. These stories can incorporate the founders' struggles and successes. For example, a company that values initiative will retell stories of employees who went above and beyond or used creativity to solve a business problem or meet a customer need.

Values Tension and Cultural Complexity

It is common to feel that our own values are so universal that everyone should hold them. That is so for religious, political, or ethnic/cultural groups where values are considered core and not open to debate (in the religious sense, this might include a belief that they arise from a supreme being). Within a culture of like-valued people, we want everyone to share our values and may even confront others who are seen as being different.

However, living in an interconnected, global world, where people of many cultures gather, we will inevitably come upon someone whose values are different. This can even happen within a family. When children are educated, begin work, live in different places, and choose people from different cultures as their spouses (and this happens to some degree within most families), we discover values differences even among those closest to us.

Just as we sometimes experience tension between some of our personal values, the same phenomenon arises within groups. Tension arises when we experience someone close to us who acts differently than we would. In a family, for example, differences about a value of "relaxation" will be easily apparent; some members may find going to a museum revitalizing, while another group wants to stay home and play video games, and others want to get outdoors for a long hike. In business, value differences might be related to risk tolerance, environmental conditions and social impact, new products, or short- and long-term horizons.

Actively exploring values differences is important to creating high-performance teams and organizations. The more aligned and connected group members are to the values, the more they *want* to engage with activities of the group. Sometimes, a person does not fit into a group because of their values differences. To resolve such conflicts, organizations have begun to define their values and make them explicit, so those who choose to work there can see in advance if their values are compatible. This clarity creates a stronger foundation for engagement and commitment and brings the right people into the group.

For example, a culture that values and rewards teamwork can have a hard time with an individual who highly values competition and wants to win at all costs. A perfectionist will not connect with a team that likes to cut corners to get things done quickly. Being explicit about the values of an organization helps draw employees who are already aligned with them, ready to contribute to the shared mission and purpose.

The work to resolve value differences can be difficult. We can easily think that we are "right" and those with different values are "wrong" because our preference is important to us and theirs is not. We all need to remember that we feel most comfortable with others who share our values and least comfortable with those who have dramatically different ones. You won't be surprised that bridging such gaps begins with a mutual conversation to understand the circumstances and experiences that shaped these values, resulting in a greater appreciation for how their values have emerged from their divergent life experiences. It's important that we recognize differences in values and discuss them, not try to convert or condemn those who are different.

Stay curious!

One problem in families, teams, and organizations that are working to align around values is that they become less curious and open to questions and new ideas. When a group strictly enforces a values credo, it risks excluding those who want to challenge the group's shared view. Challenges to a group's values can be treated as either an irritation that is removing focus from the group (or, in extreme cases, a danger to their existence) or can be treated as an opportunity for exploration and growth. We're not advocating that you change a group's values whenever someone new comes on board, but rather to stay curious and open. When an organization says, "We hire those who share our values," it may be enforcing conformity by ruling out those who are just different—and losing out on the opportunity to have enriching discussions that lead to further innovation and agility about what the group wants to achieve and how to achieve it.

Maintaining Both Personal and Shared Values

For much of human history, culture fits neatly within spiritual/religious traditions that were held as core foundations and upheld by community leaders. People, organizations, and groups were expected to abide by these common values. There was little room for uniqueness, diversity, or negotiation. In that environment, individuals had no need to further define their personal values or life purpose—they already knew who they were and where they stood. The dominant culture was far stronger and more overpowering than individual choices and left relatively little room for the kind of values choices we are being asked to consider in this time of cultural complexity.

But today most people live in places where they coexist with multiple cultures, religions, moral codes, and models for a good life. Each group we belong to can embrace different values and shared purposes. So, the challenge for each of us is to find a way to maintain our personal identity and values while supporting the shared values of the multiple communities we belong to.

It's important to remember that while we all are part of many value-based communities, we are not fully defined by any of them. Maintaining a separation between our personal values and the smaller set of values we share with a group provides a distinction that allows an individual to have some personal values not expressed in their family, team, or organizational environment. Having a separation between these two areas provides a respectful space for individuals to be responsible for expressing their personal values and releases the team, family, or organization from needing to be responsible for the fulfillment of all the members' values.

This difference between shared and individual values is especially important in families running a business together. Business families always have members who express different values orientations—but at the same time, they may agree on core family values. Personal values do not need to overlap exactly with family values, but must be in enough agreement that everyone feels that they can fit comfortably in the culture, providing a shared foundation to discuss behavior and expectations. So, having a family values framework does not mean that everyone has *just* those values. Rather, a shared Values Statement defines the core values the family shares as the preferred way to behave. Each person then can find ways within their own personal territory to implement those values.

Dealing with Disconnects

Individuals strive to overcome conflicts that arise between their own values and those of others in their family, team, organization, or community. A person can fit comfortably and be aligned with the shared values of the group or feel disconnected and alienated from them. The concept of "fit" expresses how comfortably your personal values connect to your family or community.

Albert Hirschman, a prominent social scientist, offers a framework for people to use when they consider challenging circumstances that reflect values differences. He sees three options for responding to values tensions:[7]

- **Exit:** withdraw participation; leave the organization or community.
- **Voice:** offer feedback about the disconnect; express your differences but remain in the group.
- **Loyalty:** maintain affiliation and commitment, submerging your concerns.

These options frame the choices for individuals, teams, families, and organizations to formulate their responses to challenges. They can be used as single strategies or in combination. As an employee or family member, which strategy do you adopt? Having a clear idea of individual, team, family, and organizational values can support unwinding these tensions and conflicts. These three paths offer a way for members to distance themselves, to express dissatisfaction, or to remain quietly loyal. In our experience, however, a path of total loyalty makes it difficult to have a resilient or flexible culture and stifles collaborative change.

Shared Values Define a Culture

As we have seen, just as an individual can be distinguished by the values they stand for and live by, a strong inspiring culture that everyone is aligned around

---

7   Albert O. Hirschman, *Exit, Voice, and Loyalty: Responses to Decline in Firms, Organizations, and States* (Harvard University Press, 1970).

motivates and inspires people to take collective action. Those values will be expressed with different behaviors and should support shared goals and strategies. They will be reflected in the policies, practices, and governance of the larger group so members can draw guidance from these principles.

For a culture to be vibrant, the stakeholders—family members, employees, owners, leaders, partners—need to be in alignment with these cultural values, or they need to take one of the three pathways described earlier: exit, voice, or loyalty.

The following chapters offer a roadmap and guidance for a Learning Journey whereby families (especially those that share ownership of a family enterprise), teams, associations, and organizations identify and articulate the values that distinguish their purpose and mission to create cultural alignment. The examples and actions we present are not so much about *defining* the values as they are about *using* the values as a path to greater success in teams, organizations, and families.

CHAPTER 6

Why Families Should Identify Shared Values

Are you part of a multigenerational family business facing divergent ideas about what is best for the business and how to live their lives? This chapter and the next (as well as Learning Journey #6) explore how families can formulate shared values and use them as the foundation to design their future together. This work is essential for business families who want to share values, purpose, and mission.

The Family Is More Than the Business

A business family is not a typical family. We commonly define "family" as our household—parents and growing children, with grandparents nearby. Families are formed to raise children, who, once they reach adulthood, go out and start their own families. Families can fragment with divorce and remarriage and sometimes create blended households.

A business family, however, adds a second dimension to the nature of "family." Such families tend to stay together across generations. A business family (or family enterprise) contains generations of related people or even several families that not only have a familial relationship but also share ownership of multiple assets, investments, a business, and perhaps a family foundation. As business partners, they are tied together by trusts and other forms of shared ownership. Family members grow up immersed in the family, but they may not fully understand why they are together as business partners, what that means, or how they share this commitment. They live in a business as well as a family and must manage relationships in both. It's not easy and can lead to conflict. In these situations, adults do not move on to seek their individual paths in life, but remain connected as lifetime partners. They must learn to work and live together. Depending on their history as a family, that is not always easy.

Navigating Extended Family Legacy

These extended families find themselves as business and financial partners—tied together by their legacy. But is that all they are? The answer is no. An extended family with a legacy business forms a **community** that does more than just oversee their family enterprise; it has a reality and a set of practices all its own. Its members grew up with legacy values they stand for as a family. But as the family grows and evolves, and includes more people with varying personal values and interests, do they want to stay together? Does the center of shared values continue to hold? Members of the now-larger family ask each other, "Do we have a shared core of values that can motivate and inspire us for a new generation?" Each family enterprise, as a new generation matures, must redefine their family culture.

Maintaining energy in these legacy partnerships requires that the members find a deeper purpose and meaning for being together. In addition to sharing partnership in owning valuable assets, many members want to add deeper meaning to their family life. They renew and sustain this deeper purpose and connection by defining shared values.

The family values and purpose can then be used to set an agenda of what the growing family does together. Their values define how they will be together, what they want to do, and how they will do it. Ideally, extended families with legacy businesses build loving relationships, invest together, have fun together, own vacation properties, take vacations, learn and grow together, serve the community, and help each other out in business and life.

No matter the configuration or number of generations, values must be part of the fabric of the family that owns a company or shares wealth through investments. Like the business, a family stands for something; these values are usually held as part of the legacy from earlier generations. A family's values may include preserving traditions, developing the capability of each new adult, and serving the community—values that are relevant regardless of whether there is a business involved. That's why work on shared family values is separate from work on shared business values. As two separate (but overlapping) entities, the business and the family can have different values.

Articulating shared family values can inspire a lifetime partnership, leading to alignment of diverging interests about the wealth their family has created, what they want to do with it together, and how to sustain a common family identity across generations. Common values make it easier to agree on decisions and take action with confidence.

Wealth is not enough: values, purpose, and mission bind families together.

While any family can share values and do things together, business families with substantial assets are tied together as partners in what can be a large and complex set of responsibilities. Its members are born into this complex partnership for better or worse.

The "gift" of a thriving business offers the family a special opportunity to do things together: It provides an opportunity to engage in shared activities—managing assets, learning and growing as they navigate various challenges, or serving the community. But often, there will be division among family members about how to use and manage those resources.

- Some owners want a financial return on their investment—and little more.

- Some want the family enterprise to express their personal purpose.

- Others want to simply sustain the family legacy and traditions.

As a new generation emerges, with siblings becoming adults and new people marrying in, and as the family determines how adult children will share the resources and responsibilities of the enterprise, *the business family members will decide whether their shared wealth is enough to keep them together as a group.*

Many times, the answer is no. Wealth alone does not create unity and can often have the opposite effect. That's why many successful business families consider another question as they cross generations: do we have a strong enough purpose to remain together, and, if so, what is worth doing together? As they make decisions about how to use their wealth and what to do with their shared assets, family members often decide to create a common foundation for doing something important and meaningful by identifying and reinforcing shared family values. Its members draw on values, purpose, and mission to create a way to express shared engagement and impact, as Rupert Phelps notes in the 2023 book, *Family Office Fundamentals.*

Governance needs to be based on values, purpose, and mission. Those three words are in that deliberate order.

Values come first because they rarely change. Or at least it is unusual for them to change. When you are helping a family with governance, it is foolish to expect individuals—whether they number four or forty—to have the same values. And it is equally foolish to try and change them so that they are a better fit for one another. You cannot get something like a family constitution (a document outlining the shared policies, agreements, and practices of a business or financial family) without thoroughly understanding a family's values at a personal and collective level. They are the absolute bedrock of someone's worldview.

Second is purpose. Purpose is about reaching the goals founded on the values. But of course, because things evolve and change, those goals can change too. In fact, they may never be reached. But like effective family governance, the process in itself should be beneficial, especially if it's ably facilitated, whether by a family member or a professional. It's like the athlete training before the race: the training itself is of benefit, irrespective of outcome.

Finally, there is mission. This is the end goal, which the purpose is seeking. For example, eradicating malaria or preserving a specific amount of wealth for, say, the sixth generation. Like the purposes of which it's made up, the goal may never be reached. But also, like the purposes, the means can matter more than the ends.[8]

Together, these elements—values, mission, and purpose—help a family make sense of its connections, providing generational coherence and stability. They also help forge inspiration and generate shared action. This connection forms the core of a Family Values Statement and helps them tell the story about where they have come from, who they are, what they are about, and what they want to be. These elements need to be reaffirmed regularly, especially as a new generation emerges. Each family generation faces different conditions and needs to adapt and grow to remain vital in changing environments.

The Values Advantage for Family Businesses

Family values in a business family are not the same as their business values, though they are often connected. Many families choose values—such as respect, collaboration, attention to interconnectedness, quality, and honesty—that are implemented differently in the family from the way they are in their business.

---

8 Mark Somers, *Family Office Fundamentals: Human Capital Matters* (Independent Publishing Network, 2023). Rupert Phelps is quoted on pages 104–105.

But the family's values are often attractive to employees of the business, and the willingness of the family to support these values consistently is a differentiator of family businesses.

One aspect of a family business that can make it competitive for attracting top talent is that, with a family in control, the company can often sustain a long-term commitment to values and can be depended upon to adhere to them because of the family's stewardship and its ability to look beyond the immediate bottom line. In a classic example, when Malden Mills, a New England-based manufacturer of textiles, had a huge fire that destroyed three of its four manufacturing buildings, the family owner was celebrated for pledging not to lay off workers while the factory was rebuilt. He put his company at risk to fulfill this pledge, placing values above the bottom line. Other family-owned companies visibly keep to their values even within a difficult business environment. As family owners they frequently have the resources to do this, and their stated values allow them to make these choices.[9]

Knowing a company stands for something, such as the quality of its products, is an important selling point to build trust between owners, employees, customers, and the community. Recently, the concept of the B Corp or "Social Benefit" Corporation has become another governance model for keeping family values in a business. They are businesses that do more than make a profit. There are over 2,000 for-benefit companies in the United States and Canada certified by B Lab to meet high standards of social and environmental performance, accountability, and transparency, demonstrating a commitment to benefiting all stakeholders, not just shareholders.[10]

---

9   The willingness to make sacrifices and incur costs to serve values is a quality that is common in family businesses, as noted, for example, in research such as that presented in Dennis Jaffe's book, *Borrowed from Your Grandchildren: The Evolution of 100-Year Family Enterprises* (Wiley, 2021).

10 See B Lab to learn more about this certification: https://www.bcorporation.net/en-us/.

Values Provide a Touchstone During Transitions and Renewal

The following scenario is very common for families that run a business:

The XYZ family is at a crossroads. After a generation of owning a hugely successful business, the six members of the second generation are growing in their own ways. Two of them work for the manufacturing business and one other sibling manages the family's growing real estate holdings. The other members are professionals raising their own families.

This transition leads them to ask the following questions:

- Do we all want to continue to own this business?
- What do we want to do together?
- What do we want to do individually?
- How are we a group, rather than a group of related households?
- How can our family support us as a group?

Such questions can lead to a series of conversations, focused on shared and individual values, and allow a family to make consequential decisions about business practices. At this stage, some families liquidate their assets, divide their wealth, and allow each household to go its own way. But others pause and engage in a regenerative conversation about what a foundation of shared values and assets might make available to the shared enterprise/ecosystem in which families can have a long-lasting positive impact.

Predictable Times for Refreshing Shared Values

If you are part of a successful family enterprise, you likely have legacy values that originated with the founding generation. But family enterprises experience common predictable points of transition and change that trigger the need to revisit their values. Here are some common examples:

- **Children grow into new roles:** In doing so, some may feel a disconnect with the enterprise's founding values. If, for instance, a family values treating everyone equally in terms of sharing resources, this can discourage a young family member who feels that his or her contribution to the family should be more richly rewarded.

- **There may be the desire to find new ways to benefit society:** Many business families look at their successful legacy of creating wealth or their reputation for building an enterprise, catalyzing community improvements, or becoming known for a collective mission and purpose, and in the process discover renewed energy from working together to build the next chapter of their enterprising family.

- **New people enter or leave the family:** As new members marry into the family and siblings grow up to form their own households, the family has an opportunity to redefine who they are. New people have new ideas, and the legacy values can be referenced to see how they can support these new interests. To continue as an active family enterprise, the new generation needs to define who they are, why they are together, what they are doing, and how they are going about it.

- **Generational transition and succession:** While the business founders or current leaders look ahead to future generations and wonder what is next for them, the incoming generations will naturally identify new challenges and have personal values that they want to express through the family business. The new generation will most likely want to know that these emerging concerns will be addressed while the older generation will probably have an interest in preserving the culture that has made the company successful thus far.

- **Major economic, social, and environmental disruption:** Major events happen all the time, and the family enterprise must be prepared to deal with everything from upturns or downturns in the economy to shifts in customer demands to changes in society or their physical environment.

The need for renewal may also be initiated with the death of a key person or leader, the sale of the legacy business or major asset, or a large business shortfall or reversal.

· **Key decisions about growth and direction:** Some family members may want the enterprise to expand or broaden its focus, while others may want to maintain the status quo.

At these key transition points, families benefit if they reexamine why they are together. Over the generations, an "enterprising family" must define clearly what it has been and what it wants to be in the future. Defining a shared core purpose emerges from a series of conversations that explore how a business family acknowledges their past, embraces current environments, and builds a vision for their future.

· What has been the legacy of the family?
· What do they want to become over the next generations?
· What do they want to be known for beyond their wealth?
· What do they want to do together as a family?
· What do they want to build for the family legacy?
· What will support the family culture beyond their family business?
· What will inspire and motivate the family to do things together?

Discussing these questions will help family members find answers about whether to remain a family of business partners and, if so, what that means and how to do it.

Revising and refreshing core values provides a strong foundation for renewed commitment and continuity. The legacy values have served the family, but the new conditions and the presence of new adult family members create the need for a reset. Renewing shared values is a good way for the family to get to that core purpose. It comes from analyzing what they do well and who they have been, and defining what emerging values they want to see expressed and embodied in their shared activity. They begin with the legacy values but often add some new features and emphases.

Public Families Need Values Statements

As an example of how families redefine their values across generations, a number of long-term, very wealthy families have sold or moved beyond their legacy business. After being owners of an influential business, the new generation shifts into the new role of being important stewards in the broader ecosystem of their community, taking active roles in politics and civic engagement. They are often featured in the media and face scrutiny from the community about what they do. They then become a *public* family known for its community leadership, social prominence, and public service.

As these families evolve from owning a legacy business into a visible social institution, they increasingly define themselves through the emerging family values of each new generation. And since it is a public family, they differentiate and define who they are by different shared values than those of their legacy business. The family might have many new members with very different interests. Such families often come to agree on certain values they stand for, which they announce to the whole community. In doing so, they ask to be held accountable for them.

One example of how public families demonstrate their influence is through the **Giving Pledge**. Originated by Bill Gates, Melinda French Gates, and Warren Buffett, the Giving Pledge is a shared public commitment by a wealthy family to give more than half their wealth to philanthropy. Those who sign the Giving Pledge publish a letter in which they define the values and purpose behind their gifts.[11] These letters, penned by more than two hundred fifty families around the world can be read on the group's website. They describe the values of families that control nearly a trillion dollars of global wealth.

---

11 See "About the Giving Pledge," https://givingpledge.org/about and "Pledge Signatories," https://givingpledge.org/pledgers.

The Rockefeller family, for instance, now in its sixth generation, has evolved from owning the largest oil company in the United States to becoming a values-based extended family with two hundred members and a wide variety of investments, invested according to social impact values. Soon after its first generation, the family differentiated itself from its history with the oil business and redefined itself with a service and values orientation. The five Rockefeller brothers who made up the third generation declared their values as a partnership among a network of households, each of which has a core identity in service and philanthropy. In its fourth generation, the family affirmed values it held for the members' shared efforts:

> Nurture family through the generations, provide safe environments for open dialogue, respect diversity, consider every topic within a larger context, think long-term, serve effectively with your communities, support the value of leadership and public service, and do not take yourself so seriously.[12]

The Strong Glue of Family Values

Any extended family—including but not limited to those who run a business— must, from time to time, review and redefine their shared values separate from values they may use to operate a business. These shared family values are a strong glue that can keep the family engaged and committed to accomplishing collective goals together, no matter what form they take.

---

12 From public statements and books produced by the family, quoted from Dennis T. Jaffe, *Borrowed from Your Grandchildren: The Evolution of 100-Year Family Enterprises* (Wiley, 2020), 53.

CHAPTER 7

Identifying and Implementing Shared Family Values

Companies can seek out and hire people who share their values, but families do not have that option—and so, in some ways, families have the opportunity for more diversity of thought. When family members disagree strongly, they cannot avoid each other; they must work out the differences. Discussing values as a family can help draw attention to common aspirations and provide guidance for making decisions about joint endeavors, whether that be a business or some other effort.

The values of the business family lie in two areas:

1. The quality, nature, and purpose of relationships family members want with each other.

2. The purpose, direction, and governance of the shared enterprise.

This chapter and Learning Journey #6 focus on the first element—the values that shape family member relationships. Discussions around business values will be covered in Chapters 8 through 11 and Learning Journey #7.

Components of a Family Values Statement

To define their shared values and what they mean, business families (or indeed, any family) can use the steps in the Learning Journey (the next chapter) to develop a **Family Values Statement**. This statement provides a map for next-generation members to commit time and energy to being part of the family enterprise. These shared values shape an agenda of activities, practices, and meaningful work for the family enterprise.

A Family Values Statement has three elements:

1. A broad summary paragraph expressing the family's core values/principles.
2. Definitions and explanations of what each value means and how the family will express it.
3. Structures and policies for applying the values to business and family practices.

The statement integrates several types of values relevant to families: reflecting the past, present, and future:

Past → Present → Future

Legacy values → personal values → current operational values → aspirational values

- **Legacy values** are those held by the older generation (likely the wealth creators)—the matriarchs and patriarchs whose success initiated the family business. These are values the founders held when they built the initial business.
- **Personal values** of older and younger individuals reflect their unique preferences and circumstances.
- **Current operational values** define the family as a group and are linked to actions and goals that individuals cannot achieve on their own.
- **Aspirational values** inspire the family to build something together for future generations, something that will continue to manifest the hopes and visions of the family.

Multigenerational families renew their ongoing commitment to their families by differentiating these four kinds of values. The intent is to build greater understanding and commitment to evolving goals and circumstances.

Values Reflect Actions, Not Words

Keep in mind that values are not *created* by a Values Statement—the values already exist. Rather, a Values Statement merely recognizes the ones that exist and validates them in a public way. That's because values define what the family does, not what they say!

Examples of Family Values Statements

The Family Values Statement provides an anchor for individuals, teams, and the whole family to assess how they are upholding those values. To show how these elements come together, we present two examples from two different types of families. The first is from a family that owns a growing chain of specialty stores. The second is a much more expansive expression of family values generated by a fifth-generation manufacturing enterprise.

Example 1

This family owns a growing chain of novelty stores, as well as real estate and a family office. The third-generation family members have many interests and values they want to embody in their enterprise.

> *We have worked together for nearly four generations building several businesses and supporting each other to work together and to follow our own passions in life. Underlying our partnership, we have held to several core principles:*
>
> **Family:** *A place of unconditional love where individuals develop and grow with the support, assistance, and a foundation for others in the family unit. Fun times, personal connections, tough times, joy, happiness, crisis—full of emotional presence. Honest communication. Lift and build. Constructive and instructional direction/redirection given to individuals and to the family. Recognize the importance of the individual within the family.*
>
> **Work ethic:** *Always give your best in action, words, and service. Be known as the one who shines, can be open in communication, have a smile on your face through the good and challenging times. Be reliable, punctual, prepared, and educated.*
>
> **Integrity:** *Foster, cultivate, and teach to family generations that this is earned—not simply given.*
>
> **Balance:** *Hobbies, activities, family, friends, spouse, and children—time set aside. Self-improvement aside from work and the family. Physical,*

emotional, and spiritual balance. Service—community, church, organizations.
Philanthropy. Education. Teaching and learning.

Engaged: *By being engaged in anything that we choose to do, we are*
attempting to give it our best in every way. We recognize when things go right,
wrong, or otherwise. We lean into the discomfort and feel it. We take it all in,
try to digest it, and then react in a connected manner.

Example 2

This is from a fifth-generation manufacturing family who built their business
over two generations. After the fourth generation took over leadership, and the
fifth generation expressed a desire to be included as well, this family convened
several sessions to define and articulate not only what their values were, but also
what they meant. The values work was part of a larger family strategy when the
family felt it needed a revised mission, vision, and set of values.

Task forces were created to work on these issues. The values task force asked
each family member to choose values that pertained to the family and the company. They collected and refined the responses and then rolled the revised list out
to the larger family at the Annual Family Assembly, where the full group approved
them. The task force added definitions of the values, proposed anti-values, and
gathered stories to make each value clearer. They used it to inspire each family
member to step up to stewardship.

Figures 7.2 to 7.6 represent the highly formalized family statement that
evolved from several years of a structured, sponsored effort across generations
and geographies. The meetings involved opportunities to tell stories about how
the values were embodied in the founding generation and how they evolved over
time. Ten years after the initial version, the family revised the values to ensure
they were still accurate, since the new fifth generation was now involved. The
values were edited slightly and approved again by the Family Assembly, demonstrating they have stood the test of time. The family graciously allowed us to
reprint them here.

Inclusiveness

DEFINITION

Comprehending stated limits or extremes.

Broad in orientation or scope.

Covering or intended to cover all items, costs, or services.

FAMILY VALUE

Each individual is part of the glue that binds our family together, and we value each person's uniqueness. We appreciate, respect, and foster diversity of thought in order to build a culture of trust and encourage the potential for creative solutions.

ANTI-VALUE

Exclusionary Decision-Making | Only A Few Make Decisions | Only One Event Throughout The Year | You're Either "In" Or You're "Out"

INCLUSIVENESS STORY

"There are multiple ways for the family to engage with the board, management and family (e.g. Family Camp, baseball game, quarterly webinars with the CEO and CFO, task forces, business unit trips). The family leadership is passionate about finding meaningful ways for the family to contribute at their comfort level and in alignment with their interests, passions and purpose. One example from this year was adding a yoga session at the Family Assembly Meeting. G. was able to serve the family in something he is passionate about and it added so much value to the meeting to have him facilitate the session. Another example is hosting the outing activity every year, as we get to see and engage with family members we might not see throughout the year, otherwise."

Stewardship

DEFINITION

The office, duties and obligations of a steward.

The conducting, supervising, or managing of something, especially the careful and responsible management of something entrusted to one's care.

FAMILY VALUE

We promote the careful and responsible management of the family, business, community, and the natural environment, all of which have been entrusted to our care for future generations.

ANTI-VALUE

Greed | Self-Aggrandizing | Promotion Of Individual Over Group Needs

STEWARDSHIP STORY

"This year, our family lived out the value of stewardship. Some examples of good stewardship are the establishment of a legal partnership for the Development and Education Fund, the Voting Trustee changes, the potential acquisition of a company that has a connection to stewardship of the environment, expanding our family governance to include non-family members, and the way that changes are communicated to the family. The family has honored the value of stewardship in the way that careful and thoughtful transitions have been made in family governance, the board and the company, always with long-term perspective in mind."

Figure 7.2: Inclusiveness

Figure 7.3: Stewardship

Transparency

DEFINITION

The quality or state of being transparent.

Transparent - free from pretense or deceit; easily detected or seen through; Readily understood; Characterized by visibility or accessibility of information, especially concerning business practices.

FAMILY VALUE

We foster a culture of transparency. We believe that explicit communication builds implicit trust.

ANTI-VALUE

Closed | Need To Know | Locked Down Information

TRANSPARENCY STORY

"The value of transparency is one that we repeat continuously. Every year, we encourage the management to give an honest view of the health of the company at the Family Assembly meeting. Sometimes the news is good, and sometimes the news is bad, but we don't shy away from telling that news because of our value of transparency, which builds trust. One story from the past year in which we successfully lived out the value of transparency was the news of a potential acquisition being shared with the family. Additionally, this year the family honored the value of transparency by increasing the financial information that is reported to the family each quarter. It is a risk to choose transparency, but we choose to do it because it builds implicit trust."

Empowerment

DEFINITION

Authority or power given to someone to do something.

The process of becoming stronger and more confident, especially in controlling one's life and claiming one's rights.

FAMILY VALUE

We are committed to creating and cultivating opportunities for growth and education. We acknowledge the value and necessity of taking calculated risks. Learning from mistakes and expressing forgiveness and compassion

ANTI-VALUE

Dictatorship | No Resources | Lack Of Opportunity | Keeping Down | Unforgiving, Calloused, Holding Grudges

EMPOWERMENT STORY

"The family feels so strongly about empowerment through education that we sent several family members to the Family Business Stewardship Institute at XXX University. This speaks volumes about the family's commitment to the growth and development of future generations. The establishment of the Development and Education Fund, and the family's continued participation, affords every member of the family, regardless of financial status, the opportunity for self-empowerment through family business education. Ultimately, this empowers the greater family to be the best possible partner to the management and board."

Figure 7.4: Transparency

Figure 7.5: Empowerment

Relationships

DEFINITION

The state of being related or interrelated.

The relation connecting or binding participants in a relationship.

A state of affairs existing between those having relations or dealings.

FAMILY VALUE

We agree that the quality of our relationships with each other, ideal, outside resources, and our community ensure our continued success. Our relationships go beyond legal obligation, to a commitment to strengthen future generations, maintain personal connections, and create lasting memories

ANTI-VALUE

Family Members Operating Independently | Without Connection To One Another | Failure In The Execution Of Our Other Values

RELATIONSHIPS STORY

"Developing meaningful relationships is important to all family members, regardless of age. But, the critical group that we need to develop meaningful relationships is the G5s. Putting that diverse group of kids together for long days of semi-proctored play causes the normal squabbles and bad decisions. However, the normalization of, and resolution to squabbles will go a long way to helping the G5s develops meaningful relationships with one another and will lay a solid foundation for helping them manage through conflict and challenges as adults."

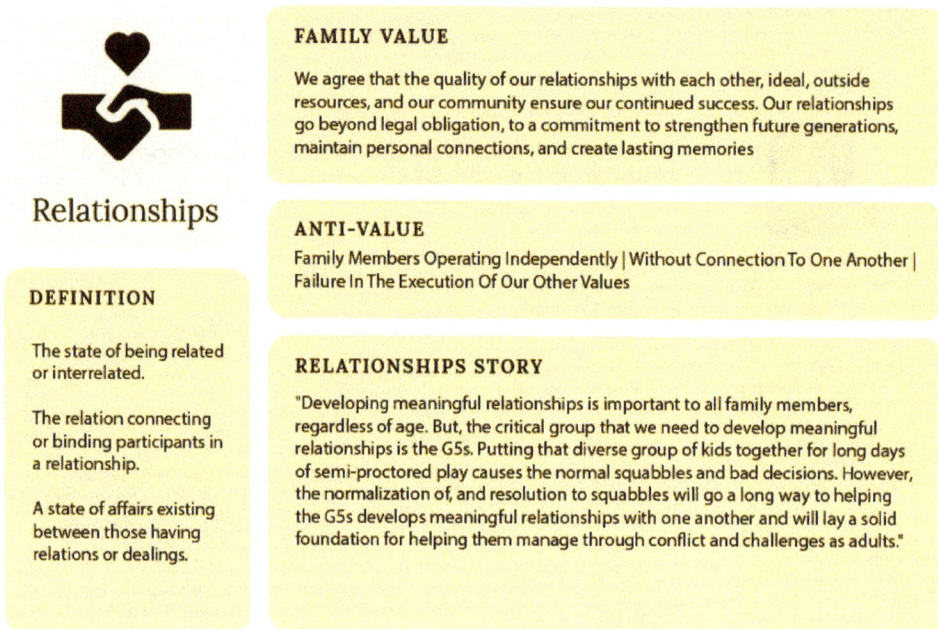

Figure 7.6: Relationships

Why Create a Family Values Statement?

Values are tangible; the ones these families chose led to deeper reflection about why the family came into being, who they are now, and who they want to become. These values define the family and can engage family members who want to remain connected to the larger family culture or repel others who wish to separate from it and move on. A statement of shared family values provides a beacon for guiding choices and actions as families navigate challenges.

Taking time to develop a Family Values Statement increases the likelihood that the values identified by the family will be considered when they face major decisions. The statements also allow people to connect observable behaviors to values and to discuss disconnects between what a person says they value and what they are actually doing. This feedback about a perceived gap between current action and espoused values encourages clarification and adjustment, so trust and respect can be restored.

As values are constantly changing and evolving, it's important that each generation has a hand in revising the shared values as part of understanding who they have been and who they want to be in the future. Having a compelling Values Statement is a key component in encouraging family members to stay connected and engaged across generations. Understanding the legacy, current, and emerging values provides a living framework for cross-generational connection.

Bringing the Family Together to Work on Values

The process of going from diverse opinions about values to a Family Values Statement like the examples shown earlier takes much more effort than picking a few words to include on a website. Creating a shared Family Values Statement is a collaborative, collective process with many voices to be heard and many viewpoints to consider.

It is common for families to have multiple rounds of discussions that include people across generations, and ongoing analysis of the numerous individual values brought forth to identify clusters and patterns that can be used to create a more simplified set of shared principles that can represent the whole family's values. This process commonly goes through multiple drafts and revisions before a Family Values Statement emerges.

Since family values belong to an extended family, the Learning Journey following this chapter describes eight steps that a smaller (first- and second-generation) family can go through with leadership from their own group. For larger families, a trained facilitator is useful to manage the coordination and continuity between generations and branches. It can be very helpful to have a trusted guide to navigate the predictable tensions and communication challenges that often emerge when the purpose and meaning of the family are called forward.

Following are some tips to make sure that the effort put into bringing the family together will be successful.

Involving Multiple Generations

Families vary in size and number of generations. First- and second-generation family groups can usually sit around a single table, while extended third- and later-generation families may consist of scores of people in many households. Families at this larger, more complex stage might select a smaller group of representatives to work on their values; this group, in turn, can seek out and incorporate the many voices that make up the extended family. Values work gets more complex as the family includes more generations.

Depending on their size, a family values exploration can begin in two ways:

- **With the whole family together across generations.** Smaller families can meet as one group and start by affirming and celebrating the legacy values of the elders. They can then add other values from rising-generation family members who relate to the present and future of the family. These family meetings can be very impactful as new members learn their history and look to the future. They are not without controversy, because some shared values can be hard to define or are viewed differently by different members. Each value must be defined and discussed. The resulting Values Statement may go through several drafts and include explanations about what they mean.

- **Larger families guided by a steering committee.** If the extended family is larger than ten or so family members, they may be better served by naming a steering committee to work on drafting the values. An optimal size is four to seven members. If there are several family branches, they might select one or two from each branch. This core representative group must communicate with the rest of the family regularly, before and after each meeting, to share what was done and get further input. This hub-and-spoke model connects many individuals to the whole process. In the end, the whole family validates the Values Statement and supports the creation of policies and processes inspired by them.

Start by Identifying Personal Values

Personal values belong to each individual and arise from personal internal reflection. Family values belong to an extended family and are partly built by dialogue among a group to discover their overlapping values. Shared family values discovery involves all family members. It's a collective process with many voices to be heard and many areas to consider. It's not quick or easy; it takes time to do it right. Family members may find it hard to understand what the others mean when they advocate different values, so the process isn't as quick or definitive as with personal values. Individuals may find that some of their personal values are not relevant to the family as a whole or not shared by others, and they should not expect all their personal values to be reflected in the shared family values.

That said, starting the development process with a discussion of individual values allows family members from the rising generation to feel they are represented and understood. For example, behaviors that connect to the values of creativity, curiosity, and challenge can all be linked to the overarching cluster of *Self-Expression*, which may be expressed in a Values Statement as a family value of innovation and entrepreneurial spirit.

Look for Patterns Among Personal Values

Shared values emerge from a series of meetings. These sequential conversations may extend over months as people take time to understand what matters to the individuals and how to consolidate it into a shared statement.

The group doing the work should gather all the values that have emerged from sharing their individual patterns and begin to consolidate them into a pattern showing where these values could contribute to broader shared interests. The eight clusters of the Values Wheel model are useful in observing where each person's individual values fall in the clusters and then helping the family formulate their values within the larger clusters.

Consolidate to Shared Values

The next step moves from individual to shared values. It starts with examining the Values Wheel or resorting the original deck of values cards (included in the Values Edge 2.0 Toolkit) to select values to guide the family in considering emerging concerns and realities, such as current environment/market conditions. The family members continue sorting the values into clusters and consolidating and weighing them to reveal shared principles. Then they develop statements that describe the meaning behind each cluster.

During this process, the family should challenge itself to think about how the consolidated values apply to different situations. Here are some examples:

- Have family members identify difficult situations (misalignment with strategy, disagreement over allocation of investments or philanthropic focus, etc.) where a specific value is challenged. Then have them discuss how that challenge has been handled in the past, and what their ideas for how the value can be held in the face of the current challenge. Does the original value still hold true or are adjustments needed?

  - For example, one family we worked with had a clear tradition of protecting the environment but was also one of the largest local real estate developers in their state. It turned out that some family members were working for community groups that were taking legal action against the downtown business association—which was headed by the patriarch of the family! This was very embarrassing and very public, with the media noting that one generation of the family appeared to be at odds with the next.

- Take a specific challenge and consider different scenarios that reflect how values should be applied. For example, family conversations about values often center around how the family allocates and adjusts its investments. Are their investments in alignment with their values or are they at cross-purposes? Do they apply to new family ventures or just the ones the family has been involved in for generations? How is this selection and allocation done? Who decides?

Observing the patterns that emerge from this analysis and talking to others about how each pattern guides their thinking can lead to principles and goals that underlie people's decisions and behavior.

Navigating the Gap Between Espoused Values and Actual Behavior

As we noted in an earlier chapter, a Family Values Statement is not ornamental. Once it is written, the family members must make sure the values are lived by. Though it is common for people to want to be seen as having strong values that correspond to ideas about what good families and leaders do, in many cases there is a gap between stated (or espoused) values and actual behavior. That is, the Values Statement expresses values that aren't necessarily backed up in action.

For example, if family leaders say they are open to ideas but then show little interest in what the other family members propose, that may reflect a lack of alignment with the espoused values of *curiosity* and *innovation*. Or a family that espouses the value of making business decisions on merit is experiencing a gap if there is an informal preference for allowing the offspring of one elder family leader to make the decisions. When any organization appears to act very differently from its values, the gap between actual and espoused values can inhibit healthy expression and constrain the organization.

Any gap between espoused and practiced values allows values tensions to surface, often along generational lines. For example, a large ranch-owning family experienced a gap in what "stewardship" of natural resources looks like, with wide differences between generations in interpreting that value. Some felt that cattle ranching reflected good stewardship, while others saw this as not sustainable. How can the family acknowledge the legacy values of the founders' ranching history with the current emphasis on reducing the land engaged in ranching? These conversations about legacy and evolving values between the generations show how values/principles can be a living framework for navigating these situations.

Dynamic Values, Dynamic Family

The goal of the work to create a Family Values Statement is not to create a "tight" agreement, but to establish a place where the family can return to find balance about what is important while still leaving room for individual expression.

A Family Values Statement will be most successful when it allows the next generation to see opportunities for influencing the direction of the family and when it is treated as a living, breathing instrument that requires regular attention. The result is a dynamic, resilient family that can navigate transitions and challenging times while holding true to the values they want to represent and uphold.

Family Values Conversations Roadmap

This Learning Journey follows an eight-step roadmap for having conversations that guide you in creating a Family Values Statement.

Previous Learning Journeys have focused on individual exploration. To engage a whole family in creating a shared Values Statement requires time and attention dedicated to making sure all parts of the family are included.

This Learning Journey describes a collective process with many voices to be heard and differences to be navigated. It is not quick or easy and requires a persistent, dedicated focus and time commitment to maintain momentum. It is iterative and goes through multiple revisions as family members ponder what the others mean when they advocate for different values. It also allows families to propose explicit activities that support each value.

This journey will feature the process for a small family, ten to fifteen members representing first-, second-, and third-generation families. Larger, more complex families, with multiple branches, complex governance, and considerable assets will be best served by having an outside consultant/facilitator to guide them.

Meeting Preparation

First and foremost, the members of the family must agree on the task and the desired outcome. They will need time and commitment to do this. All segments of the family need to be included. The family should set a time in advance and find a private and comfortable place to meet, where they can face each other—maybe in a circle, or, for a larger group in a U-shape facing the front. Having a flip chart or whiteboard in the room helps to facilitate the conversations. This work can be done by the whole family or by the designated steering committee.

Tip: Use a neutral facilitator for the process.

Because there are many moving parts, and because of the likelihood of disagreements between family members, we recommend you have a neutral, skilled, experienced facilitator (i.e., NOT a family member) to lead you through the activities described in this Learning Journey. Select a facilitator who can uphold the ground rules of the group, keep the process moving, and intervene when there are disruptions.

Roadmap for Creating a Shared Family Values Statement

Here are **action steps** for bringing the family together to define values. This is not a facilitation guide, but a roadmap for identifying and navigating the elements, topics for discussion, and sequence of tasks to help a family navigate a Shared Values Statement.

1. Complete Personal Values Pyramid
2. Personal Values Appreciation

3. Acknowledge Legacy Values

4. Explore the Current Environment

5. Identify and Prioritize Current Family Values

6. Anchor Values in Behaviors

7. Explore Emerging Values

8. Frame a Family Values Statement

1. Complete Personal Values Pyramid

We strongly recommend that everyone who attends the values conversations meetings have completed a personal values exploration and crafted their own Values Pyramid, as described in Part I. The insight and clarity each family member gains with their Personal Values Pyramid sets up a foundation for developing a shared Family Values Statement.

2. Personal Values Appreciation

After everyone has identified their personal values and priorities in their Values Pyramid (using the processes described in Part I), if the family is small enough, you can have each individual show and share their Values Pyramid with their primary and secondary drivers and talk about what is important to them. Take time to acknowledge and appreciate the diversity of values individuals bring to the family. Allow the group to notice similarities and differences and to identify major areas of convergence. Some of these differences will be because people are in different stages of their life cycles. A young married person's values are different from those of a person in their later decades.

This session helps the family acknowledge the shifting patterns related to the life cycle. There is a rich diversity of perspectives in every family that can be harnessed to give focus and alignment to decision-making.

Values Gallery Walk

One way to quickly observe the patterns of similarities and differences is to have each person place their Values Pyramid in front of their seats and then have everyone take five minutes to walk around, as if they were in an art gallery, noticing patterns of similarities and differences.

This can be followed by having each member carry on one-on-one conversations with someone who is most like them and then someone most different. Each person should explain how their values are reflected in their current life/work. This conversation serves to establish connections and understanding across generations, branches, and operational roles.

After each family member has established and shared his or her own values, the group can get together to explore similarities and differences and identify areas of convergence. The family will then have a broader understanding of the many values drivers and preferences within the family. Acknowledging the differences allows them to learn from each other and to see that, while there are many values that are important to all, everyone has a few special and personal ones that guide their lives. They also learn to be open to other values and other styles they may not have considered before.

This step builds family connection with newly married-in and new adult family members and builds cohesion across branches and generations. It is a family team-building activity.

3. Acknowledge Legacy Values

Next, move to a discussion of the **Legacy Values**—the foundation that the family has lived by and that were defined by elders and prior generations. If available, you can share a prior Family Values Statement and/or the surviving elders can talk about what values have been important to the family. Sometimes the younger generations interview the elders to hear them talk about their values and what has been meaningful to them. The elders may respond by speaking directly, or they may send a letter to the family group.

Many families already have values formulated by their founding generations, often embodied in a Values Statement for their family company. The facilitator should work with the family beforehand to collect previous Values Statements, which should be shared and discussed. Bring in examples (including stories, albums, books, and celebrations) where the family has communicated their values. Legacy values and company values are to be honored but not used as a shortcut to create the current Values Statement. Each generation is invited to remember and reaffirm the values the family has lived by and will live by.

There are several ways to do this. In one method, each person in turn shares one of the Legacy Values they feel have been important to the family. After several rounds there will be a list of maybe a dozen. The family can then identify which have been the most influential in their becoming the family they are now. This collection is integrated with the emerging values into the final Family Values Statement.

Harvesting Values Through Storytelling

Another activity that is very helpful in surfacing family values is telling family stories. This activity takes time. It can be a whole session for a family group.

Each person is asked to tell a story about the family that recalls an experience that shows the essence of one or more of the values.

There might be some order to the stories, maybe going from branch to branch, or starting with the oldest family member and going down in order of age.

After telling each story the family might summarize the behaviors actions that demonstrated this value. Using the Values Wheel and the 8 clusters may be a helpful way to combine and acknowledge multiple values to sum up the story. The result will be a set of values that come directly from the family's history and experience.

4. Explore the Current Environment

The purpose of this step is to surface some of the ongoing changes and challenges that are present in the current business environment. The family talks about their perceptions of social, financial, economic, and environmental changes and challenges, and discusses where the values may need to be reframed.

- What are they experiencing that is different today?
- How do they see this affecting the family and the business?

This discussion of what is evolving and what needs to emerge can take up a whole family session. It will inform which values may be important to keep, drop, or modify/reconsider as the family faces their future, which in turn sets the foundation for a future vision. It may be the first time the rising generation has been included in the conversation and asked what they want and what they believe.

The family can then add this clarity about what is emerging in the reality of the family's world to shape the final Values Statement.

Pausing Before the Next Step

It can be helpful to take a break after the first four steps. People often benefit from taking time to reflect, digest, and talk with others about what they have observed and experienced in hearing about personal values, Legacy Values, and the discussion about the current conditions that the family is navigating before moving into identifying and consolidating shared family values.

5. Identify and Prioritize Current Family Values

This step should be done at a separate meeting, with enough time for discussion and reflection. The goal is to have the family agree on a list of priority values (just as individuals did when developing their Values Pyramid).

The best way to develop a set of shared family values is to have people look again at the list of 64 values we identified earlier or to use the color-coded values cards included in the Values Edge 2.0 Toolkit. Going around the room, have each person in the family or on the steering committee suggest a value they feel strongly should be expressed by the family now to build strength in the emerging environment. Each person talks about why that value is important to the family. Going around the room person by person allows each person to talk and feel heard.

Record the values on a flip chart, whiteboard, or list that everyone can see. Continue going around the room until no one has values they want to add to the list. The facilitator can then ask if there are any values missing. The list of Legacy Values might be consulted and the participants asked if some of them need to be added.

To help consolidate the list, use the 8 clusters of the Values Wheel to pair or link values with some overlap or similarity in the same cluster. For example, a family might see *loyalty* and *security* as related within the legacy cluster and find a shared word, phrase, or sentence to connect both values. There may be some benefit in combining values that occur within a cluster to show the connection between groups of values. This pairing can help surface key themes.

At the end of this discussion, several values clusters will have emerged. Write down a clean list of the proposed values with the similar values listed near each other.

Now the list can be prioritized, as was done in the Personal Values Pyramids. Each person is given a set of ten stickers (or whatever number you choose) and places their stickers by a particular value or cluster on the list, indicating their preference for which ones will be most important to maintain current and ongoing viability. They can distribute their stickers however they like, for instance, putting one sticker on each of ten different values or putting two or more stickers on values they consider most important. The stickers make it very easy to identify patterns and determine which values resonate with the family.

The next step is to sort the values into a list of five to seven that indicate the core values of the whole family.

6. Anchor Values in Behaviors

A value is shorthand for a set of behaviors or actions that demonstrate that value in action. Discussing behaviors, actions, decisions, etc., that represent each value helps to make it clearer what the value stands for. It is common to envision different behaviors for each value. This can explain how there can be so much difference in perception of what values like *respect, competence, fun, responsibility,* etc., mean. This conversation can help clear up misunderstandings about what a value means. This is not a conceptual definition but the description of a specific action, policy, or conversation, that shows that value in action. The goal is not to have a "dictionary definition" of each value but to have a shared experience of a broad set of perspectives about what a single value can mean.

The family should engage in a process that explores the top five to seven values. One way is for small groups to take on each value and describe the behaviors, actions, policies, and practices that demonstrate this value is being upheld. They might give specific examples or write about what that value has meant to the family. The idea is to give more life and clarity to the value and show how it is important to the family.

After several drafts, each value should be more clearly understood. These expositions can be shared and discussed at a meeting with the whole family, where there is time for editing and discussion. The intention is to make each value a living reality. Another part of the discussion is to explore what the challenges to expressing that value are and how it is difficult to live up to. Where might the biggest challenges to upholding these values be? The goal is to develop a meaningful description and behaviors for each core value.

7. Explore Emerging Values

There is one other type of value for a family to consider. That is, what new values might the family adopt for its future that might add to the family's strength and vitality?

A useful way to introduce new aspirational values is to ask each person to look at their own values and suggest a value not currently in the list of shared values but that they feel will benefit or inspire the family to develop and grow. As in the previous activity, each person in turn proposes one value and then states why they feel that value would help the family. This leads to a robust discussion of how the family can evolve beyond its Legacy Values.

The goal is to reach an agreement on whether any new values should be added to the overall family values list or placed in a list of aspirational values to develop. This is a time to reach a consensus rather than resort to a majority-rules vote because you want everyone to fully support the decision. If the family members cannot agree on additions, then nothing should be added.

8. Frame a Family Values Statement

At the next meeting (or before it), each of the 5 to 7 values descriptions is shared, and family members can edit or add to each one. The list becomes a set of Values Statements or principles that define the family's core purpose and intention. There can then be further consideration of how the family can make that value stronger or more real to the family.

The last step is to craft a Family Values Statement that includes a description of how the current and aspirational values will be the core of the family's decisions and actions. This may require several rounds of discussion and editing to come up with a statement that can provide guidance for the future. Some families revisit the values at their annual family retreat and talk about how they are doing and what they can do to express these values more explicitly as a family.

Continue the Cycle

As we've said before, defining family values is not a one-and-done activity that has a beginning and an end. Creating a Family Values Statement provides an ongoing opportunity for reflection, refreshing, and invigorating cross-generational conversations about the past, present, and future. Values work is foundational to the strategic planning process. It is the first step in defining what the family wants to see in its future and how the family will work together as a united and aligned group. Crafting a Values Statement often begins a planning process for the family to move from its legacy business toward a family enterprise that includes a non-financial agenda to build the shared family capital—expressing the added value they can achieve together as a family.

CHAPTER 8

What Is a Values-Based Organization?

This chapter shifts focus from the family to the business. It pertains not only to family businesses but also to any business that can be grounded in values. It differentiates a values-based organization from a rules- or policy-based organization.

As employees face increasing responsibility, making more complex and far-reaching decisions, a corporate values credo can be an essential guide for behavior. Employees at every level face customers, make (sometimes costly) decisions, and deal with balancing acts between competing priorities. Previously, business focus was generated by maintaining strict procedures and standards of behavior under the control of supervisors. Today, with more empowerment and a greater sphere of autonomy for individual employees, they might be better guided by aligning their behavior with the organization's core values. If a decision fits the values, then it is right.

And right there is the key difference between a business operating under traditional design and one that has embraced a values-based approach: A values-based organization offers employees key values and principles rather than extensive procedures and expected activities.

Rather than having to consult a detailed policies and procedures manual, which cannot cover every situation, employees are trusted to consider values or principles to guide their priorities, decisions, and actions. For example, in a company that espouses a "customer first" value, when a customer or supplier has a problem or presents a special case, the employee does not have to search through a tome of policies or say, "I'm sorry, but that's against procedure." He or she can instead use judgment and creativity to improvise and fix the situation. They know what the culture stands for and make decisions based on that. This has a positive effect on all parties. It frees management up from being involved in minutiae, and it leaves the employee feeling empowered and like a respected member of the team because they resolved the problem without involving layers of approval.

In short, rather than follow procedures and rules that limit what can be done, a values-based culture empowers employees to do what is right, with the understanding that if they decide based on the organization's values, they will not be punished or second-guessed. It creates an environment where people are free to act and where the organization can benefit from their initiative. It is the opposite of a rule-based culture.

Reaching a point where you can use values and purpose to guide daily actions isn't as simple as developing a Values Statement and posting it on the wall. Every worker has to live up to a set of expectations, but the level of trust and freedom for each person to do the right thing is greater. This has many effects, as we will see. This next chapter takes an in-depth look at what it means to be a values-based organization and what it takes to create one, starting with a case study to illustrate the core idea.

J.M. Huber: A Century of Family Leadership Through Values

We begin with an example of how a company culture that stems from consistent, widely and deeply held values can motivate high performance in employees as they adapt to a continually changing business environment. They became a values-based (or purpose-based) enterprise.

The J.M. Huber Corporation was founded in 1883 by a German immigrant to New York. The enterprise has grown over the past 140 years to become a $3 billion portfolio of privately held industrial and forest-product companies. Under the evolving leadership of successive generations of the founding family and talented and dedicated non-family employees, the companies have been well managed, with a growth and acquisition orientation. They attribute their success to a deep and continual dedication to what they call the **Huber Principles**, which have evolved from core values practiced in the business's early years and continually adapted to new and emerging challenges faced by each generation.

Fifth-generation family board member Zachary Seely[13] explained how the Huber Principles are at the center of who they are and how that culture is transferred to and expressed by their thousands of employees, leaders, customers, suppliers, partners, and community members. It offers a model for how values in action are at the core of many successful family enterprises.

While non-family companies can also express and promote a culture of values, there are ways that family ownership and leadership can sustain and focus a business on values that are more difficult at a public company with scores of owners having no connection. Family enterprise values are not simply invented by a committee or task force or from an employee popularity poll. That is part of their power; they usually emerge from the long-term legacy of personal beliefs by the founding generation and their heirs.

The founders had a deep feeling for a way of doing business and a dedication to care for their products, customers, employees, organizational practices, and integrity. When a second- or later-generation family or employee group set out to define the values, they were readily inferred from how the elders ran the

---

13 Presentation in 2024 at Transitions, a semiannual event sponsored by *Family Business Magazine* that meets to share best practices by business families.

business. But by making them explicit, though, differences of opinion about what they mean surfaced.

So, when family leader Mike Huber (third generation) set out to define the Huber Principles in 1987, after a hundred years of successful operation, the values were not invented—they were already implicitly present in how the company did business. Mike wanted to make them clearer and more explicit so they could be learned and practiced by new generations of family and employees. Ten years later, Peter Francis (a fourth-generation family member) refined the five principles and expanded them to seven. He, in turn, was succeeded by Mike Marberry, a non-family leader, who further revised them down to four. In 2022, non-family CEO Gretchen McClain rephrased them again through her Vision 150 initiative:

- Safety & Sustainability
- Respect for People
- Ethical Behavior
- Excellence

These values are hardly startling or unique, but we can imagine that if a company really puts them into action, they promote a workplace where employees want to work and contribute their best.

Living the Values

For the four principles to be a guide for aligned action in a company like Huber, with many business units and employees operating worldwide, they, of course, needed fleshing out. They developed a catchphrase for each (along with more detailed descriptions you can find on their website):[14]

---

14 "Who we are and what we want to achieve is rooted in our core values," *Huber.com*, https://www.huber.com/about/the-huber-principles/.

- Safety & Sustainability: "World-class safety and environmental performance"
- Respect for People: "We welcome and treat all people with honesty, respect, and integrity"
- Ethical Behavior: "A company identity that we are all proud of"
- Excellence: "Competitive advantage through customer intimacy, innovation, and operational excellence"

The Huber family and its leadership understood that the principles are not the end goal but rather an early step in putting these values to work in a corporate culture. The Huber Principles are expressed publicly in every part of the company's operations. In public statements, each unit announces how they are doing in relation to those principles. The leaders also hold themselves accountable to a demanding public.

Every year, in addition to its **Corporate Annual Report**, Huber issues a detailed **Impact Report** about what it has done in relation to the stated values. The report goes into detail about values and partnerships, along with the initiatives, actions, and metrics of what the companies have done in relation to each of their principles. For example, the corporation gives an annual Mike Huber Award to an internal team that best expresses its values and principles. Every year, hundreds of teams from every part of the world and all their companies announce their candidacy for the award. Several teams are honored in the report, and the winning gold award team is invited to share their stories and be recognized at the annual family shareholder meeting. Employees are proud of what they do, but they seem proudest when they succeed within the framework of the Huber Principles.

The principles are linked to supporting global sustainability, safety, and diversity practices. And to benefit from the examples of other families, the company joined the World Business Council for Sustainable Development, which relates to several other groups reporting their environmental, waste, energy, safety, and diversity accomplishments. Their results show improvements in many areas that have to do with respect for their employees, their community, and the environment.

Even When It's Not Easy

The benchmarks and metrics are an ongoing challenge for Huber's chemical and industrial products companies that draw on natural resources, so those divisions continually look at their business practices and ask each employee to help the corporation reach its goals. They also look for ways to follow the four principles while remaining profitable; in so doing, the companies act as role models and share ideas for practices that can have huge social benefits. One of the divisions has even become a B Corp—a company that voluntarily meets the highest social and environmental performance standards.

The Huber Principles offer a shared language for everyone in the company, based on understanding how they work together and what they stand for. They make it safe for employees to speak up about things that need to change and suggest new ideas that add to their impact. It creates a culture in which employees want to work and feel motivated to do their best. As a result, employee retention is high, and some families have several generations that work for the company.

Huber finds many ways to support its employees: benefits that support family well-being, time for volunteer and community service, and even informal groups of employees who share common hobbies and interests and meet after-hours to pursue them together. It's no surprise that Huber is continually found on the lists of Great Place to Work.

The Huber culture places importance on storytelling rather than numbers for expressing and sharing values. Time is taken in every corporate meeting to share stories of positive things that are being done to support its values. That is how the principles have become such a strong part of the corporate DNA—everyone remembers the stories and enjoys retelling them. They also add validity and positive motivation for active engagement.

Soon to celebrate its 150th year, Huber focuses on its *Vision 150* that looks ahead several generations. While purpose-based family businesses may not be common, their success is inviting other companies to emulate what they are doing.

Thinking Long, Long Term

Values at Huber and other family enterprises are not a wall decoration or symbolic action, but a living reality that embodies the deep nature of the company. And because a family has owned the company for over 140 years and expects to continue for generations to come, it can ensure that the principles will continue to be honored.

Working in a Values Culture

At work, as in other areas of their life, people assume certain basic values, acting on them but rarely defining them clearly or questioning them. To be effective, a company needs some agreement about what it values and then needs to turn these values into policies, practices, and standards for behavior.

The trend toward a focus on values is becoming more pronounced today. Companies like Patagonia and North Face lead with their values and consider them a competitive advantage.

J.M. Huber's level of detail in Values Statements and principles is a great example of how to use those elements to set standards that should be considered in every action and business decision. For example, when conducting the business of the organization—working with a customer, defining priorities, evaluating employee performance, making tough decisions, or bringing people together—values set standards against which an individual choice or action must be measured.

Values also define ideals to which a person should hold himself or herself accountable. An employee knows, "If I act according to my judgment about the company's set of values, I am enhancing my value to the company." The values would also come into play if they were faced with an employee whose behavior seemed to contradict the values. The person might not see his or her action as contradicting the value, and this might lead to an important discussion of the meaning and purpose of a value for the organization.

A story from family-owned Nordstrom about extreme devotion to the company principle of satisfying every customer has achieved near-mythological status.[15] The story dates to the mid-1970s when a customer came into a Nordstrom store insisting on a refund for a pair of used tires. Keep in mind that Nordstrom has *never* sold tires (though this particular location was built on the site of a former tire store). The manager instructed staff to honor the return and give the customer a refund.

The story is retold as an example of heroic, unquestioning service. All Nordstrom employees learn to apply the value of customer satisfaction in individual ways, learning continually from their colleagues' new ways to achieve customer satisfaction. This core value thus leads to ongoing innovation and employees themselves creating new ways to deliver value beyond expectations.

Judgment Calls: The Leader's Role in Clarifying Values

One caveat about the Nordstrom tire story: Is it really a heroic success? Or is it an example of how misapplied values can cost the company or even undermine its basic intention? At what point should a team invest in educating a team member about the intent behind a value and when should they let it go? Extreme service might not always be a virtue!

---

15 Geoff Bright, "No Questions Asked, Even for Tires: The Nordstrom Legend That's (Surprisingly) True," *Bright Info Publishing*, November 25, 2024, https://brightinfopublishing.com/professional-success/no-questions-asked-even -for-tires-the-nordstrom-legend-thats-surprisingly-true/.

That's where the role of leaders comes in. They should have conversations with their team members to discuss real-world situations they might face and how the company's values apply. If the tire story was applicable, for example, the topic of team conversations would be whether giving a refund was the right decision or foolish and counterproductive. Such conversations are critical today, when we hear that customers take advantage of loopholes and abuse—refund or return policies, for example—so employees must use their judgment as they apply principles. Alternatives might be for the employee to talk with the customer about why they have a problem or what their real concerns are.

Loudly Define Your Intent

Values loudly define what the company stands for in its operations, products, and community. This is true of all businesses—large and small, public and private, for-profit and non-profit. But in a values-driven company, the proof should be evident in everything the company does. If you shop at Trader Joe's, you'll find that every employee is glad to stop what they are doing and help you find something on your shopping list. This is a deeply ingrained corporate value. (We are all familiar with other stores where it is impossible to find an employee or get help, or where many of the goods are locked up.)

Based on our half-century of experience, we deeply believe that an organization or business entity operates more effectively when it builds a defined culture based on shared and expressed values and allows them to make decisions about what to do from the values rather than a set of strict rules. Making values clear and explicit offers employees, and even external partners, guidance on how they are expected to make decisions about their work.

CHAPTER 9

Developing Values with a Collaborative Process

If identifying and implementing values were a simple exercise, many businesses would undertake the effort. In fact, undertaking embedding of values in the policies, processes, and culture usually arises when there is a significant challenge in quality, direction, performance, or attracting talent. There must be reasons beyond "it feels good" for an organization to invest the significant amount of time and effort it takes to develop a Values Statement and then design and implement those values.

The overall goal of clarifying organizational values is to build a strong and vital culture, where deep commitment to values, purpose, and mission builds higher levels of engagement, resulting in an organization that is more competitive in the marketplace and, if desired, more connected to its communities. The examples we present are not so much about defining the values as they are about using the values as a path to greater success in teams and organizations.

In this chapter, we'll explore a wide range of benefits your organization can gain by taking the time to develop and implement core values.

Creating Directional Beacons

As demonstrated by the Huber story in the previous chapter, core values provide the foundation for implementing an organization's strategy, mission, and structure. They are a set of understandings in an organization about how to work together, how to treat other people, and what is most important. In that way, values become a beacon that can guide employee engagement, performance, and commitment.

As the essence of a company's philosophy for achieving its goals, values provide a sense of common direction for all employees and guidelines for their day-to-day behavior.

In their influential book *Corporate Cultures: The Rites and Rituals of Corporate Life*, Terrence Deal and Allan Kennedy noted:

> If employees know what their company stands for, if they know what standards they are to uphold, then they are much more likely to make decisions that will support those standards. They are also more likely to feel as if they are an important part of the organization. They are motivated because life in the company has meaning for them.[16]

The creation of an organization aligned with a set of core values can be a powerful influence to align everyone to the core principles behind the business. An additional benefit of working toward a shared Values Statement and the deeper alignment developed in this process is the collective effectiveness that this process can generate. Alignment between values and practices forges the basis for a more conscious, intentional, generative approach to business.

Benefits of Values Alignment

A special emphasis today on clarity of values stems from several factors:

First, employees are faced with increasingly complex decisions, in increasingly

---

16 Allan A. Kennedy and Terrence E. Deal, *Corporate Cultures: The Rites and Rituals of Corporate Life* (Basic Books, 2000): 23.

ambiguous circumstances. Policies and rules cannot define or cover every situation. Often, employees come upon difficult situations and need guidance from the values to decide or act. With all this uncertainty, a company is no longer able to list rules and policies that cover every situation. And if the company tries to prescribe rules for every situation, the employee will feel diminished, distrusted, and belittled—and so will customers. How often have you asked for help and had the employee say, "I can't do that; I have to ask my supervisor"? This costs everybody. But if broad guidelines guide them, engaged, knowledgeable, and dedicated employees can figure out what to do and make the best decisions.

Second, the consequences of employee decisions are increasingly consequential, in that employees can make costly mistakes or earn the company customers and add value through timely action.

But if rules and policies can't fully tell employees what to do, what will guide them? Part of the answer stems from knowing the overall strategy, corporate mission, and goals. But another part of the answer is their values. Rather than feeling constrained by inflexible rules and policies, employees must be trusted to make thoughtful and sometimes creative decisions.

Values clarity helps a company and its employees in many other ways:

- **Motivate commitment.** Values are **motivators**, since when we feel that something is right and important, we will spend a great deal of effort to achieve it. Values can help employees find meaning and purpose in their work, care about what their company is doing, and link their individual efforts to those of the entire company. People who understand their values are more deeply motivated and effective at work.

- **Align action.** With employees having to make many complex decisions, values offer a set of guiding principles that help improve consistency in decision-making across the organization.

- **Continual improvement.** By understanding and adhering to values, an employee feels trusted and motivated, not just to do the minimum and not make mistakes but also to be able to help the organization avoid mistakes and continually do better.

· **Transcend individual conflicts.** Values provide a language and a way of understanding individual differences. They open the door for nonjudgmental acceptance of different ways of doing things. Values are powerful motivators. They represent an organizing principle for people's lives, as well as organizations.

· **Attracting better talent.** Having clearly defined business values will help you attract job candidates who will be a good fit for your organization. People seek out organizations that share and respect their personal values and allow them to work together with a positive sense of purpose. They identify with that purpose, and it leads them to want to work there and do their best.[17]

In addition, here are some research- and theory-based insights that underly the value-based approach to organizations:

· Families, organizations, and teams that have clarified their values have an easier time getting people engaged and committed, making effective decisions, and staying focused on those values.

· In 2021, nearly two-thirds of U.S.-based employees surveyed by McKinsey & Company said that COVID-19 had caused them to reflect on their purpose in life and reevaluate work.[18]

· People who have purpose have meaningful relationships in their personal life *and* at work. They are working toward something that matters to them, and they use opportunities to challenge themselves to grow and have more impact.

---

17   Naina Dhingra, Andrew Samo, Bill Schaninger, and Matt Schrimper, "Help Your Employees Find Purpose—or Watch Them Leave," *McKinsey & Company*, April 5, 2021, https://www.mckinsey.com/capabilities/people-and-organizational-performance/our-insights/help-your-employees-find-purpose-or-watch-them-leave.

18   Dhingra, Samo, Schaniger, and Schrimper, "Help Your Employees Find Purpose—or Watch Them Leave."

- Moreover, when employees feel that their purpose is aligned with the *organization's* purpose, the benefits include stronger employee engagement, heightened loyalty, and a greater willingness to recommend the company to others.

Another positive reason for emphasis on values has to do with employees' changing expectations of the workplace. In the past, work and family values were quite separate—you did not want to bring your personal world to work, while work relationships were formal and impersonal. Now, increasingly, people want a more personal environment at work. Even as we work more at home, we want to have personal connections at work—and this dates from the 1960s, when emerging work values led to employees wanting to bring their whole selves to the workplace. People who live their purpose at work are more productive than people who don't. They are also healthier, more resilient, and more likely to stay at the company.[19]

Employees working in a values-based organization feel that when they choose to apply a value in making a judgment call, they will receive the support and trust of the organization. They feel empowered to make decisions about applying policies, rather than fear that they will make a mistake and be sanctioned. They feel safe and trusted rather than watched over and second-guessed. The upshot is that they serve the organization and take initiative rather than act passively. This reduces costs and improves the organization in small steps.

Benefits of Involving Employees in the Process

You cannot *give* a team or an organization a Values Statement, though some leaders try. Values that are imposed will never become real to people. Of course,

---

19 This has been a focus of research over several decades by prominent organizational theorists, including Rosabeth Kanter, Warren Bennis, Jeffrey Pfeffer, Charles O'Reilly, Chris Argyris, Ed Lawler, and many others. While adopted by many public companies, these ideas have been especially important to family businesses, because of their personal relationships, long-term perspective, and values-based perspective.

leaders can suggest important values, but there is no substitute or shortcut for having individual teams talk about their most important values and come up with a consensus they support.

Similarly, because each of us brings our personal values to the workplace, each employee will apply shared business values in an individual way. So, gaining consensus about key values and what they mean is important for any group. There are benefits to be gained from the process above and beyond those generated by defining values.

One example of a situation where collaborative engagement is important is when dealing with a remote workforce. As more employees work from home and teams are more dispersed, the need for clear behavioral guidelines increases. If you don't spend time with your teammates or at the office, the development of shared culture becomes more problematic. Each group must find time to talk about values and agree on what they mean and where there is room for individual variation. A collaborative exploration of values makes these differences explicit and leads to a shared team agreement about them and what they mean.

Another situation where collaboration is helpful is when a group agrees on a vision and mission but lapses into conflict because different people have different opinions about how to put them into action. The work at a manufacturing plant, sales office, store, or procurement team is very different, and the values can be applied differently. Individuals and teams have divergent priorities, and differences are inevitable. Some members might want to work on their own; some want lots of interaction, while others see the workplace as an arena for personal competition and "winning" through good results.

Let's look at two examples of how a collaborative process helped an organization.

Collaborative Case Study 1

The benefits of a Values Statement lie not just in the result but in the collaborative process needed to get there.

For example, one communications company's area managers held a workshop to explore personal and organizational values. The workshop used values as a framework to build commitment and alignment between individuals, teams, and the company. The expectation was that by generating shared values, teams would be better able to resolve day-to-day hassles and act in ways that supported the entire company.

Each manager defined his or her personal values and shared them with others. Then, the participants identified values that defined high performance within their teams. After much discussion, each team developed a team Values Statement of the behaviors it wanted to see more of and less of from team members. The values weren't just simple platitudes. Indeed, after agreeing on the first four values, the group had a lively debate on the importance of second-tier values. The discussion went beyond abstract statements to specify exactly what each value meant.

The workshop led to a greater appreciation of people's different backgrounds and experiences. Participants looked at each other's key values and saw that different values were sometimes at the root of work disagreements. They talked them through and achieved some consensus on how they would be applied.

One of the division's goals was to create a virtual organization, in which people worked in teams at widely dispersed locations. After the workshop, each manager received materials and was encouraged to hold a similar workshop with his or her team. In follow-up interviews, two months following the workshop, participants were still enthusiastic about the results and gave specific examples of how it was useful. More than half of the managers had implemented (or were about to implement) the values workshop with their teams.

They reported the following key benefits:

- learning about each other
- understanding and respecting diversity and individual differences
- balancing different perspectives
- helping create a team
- overcoming conflict between people

The managers felt that the best use of the values was with team members who were in conflict or with whom managers were having difficulty. The use of values enabled team members to look at differences in a nonjudgmental way and discuss working together more effectively. They felt more comfortable and accepted when they shared the values consensus they developed together.

Collaborative Case Study 2

A division, office, or work team may want its own set of values. They can build on or begin with the company values, but the team finds it useful to define its own cultural values and practices apart from the organization.

Here is an account of a team defining its values together:

Around tables in a large meeting room, the 200 top worldwide managers of the largest division of a global manufacturing company were selecting their key personal values from a deck of 50 values cards. Each person arranged the cards according to his or her most important and least important values and then placed his or her name card on the piles. Next, the whole group walked around the room looking at each array. People were amazed at the diversity of the values and at the range of values people selected as most important. They could begin to understand how the values lay behind each manager's work style. Each table then had a rich discussion on how their values led them to act the way they did at work.

Next, each table came up with 7 core values that they felt should be adopted by the whole division. There were lively debates about which ones were most important for their work and were essential to continued high performance. Each table then shared its proposed values with the whole group. A recorder wrote the common values on a flip chart at the front of the room and tallied the most frequently named ones. Next, a company leader shared his core values and the thoughts behind them. The whole group then worked to develop a set of shared values. Last, small groups worked with each core value to create a Values Statement that reflected their understanding and application of each value to their work.

Participants didn't stop there. Several participants used the workshop's design and values cards to lead their own teams in a similar values discussion.[20]

This company was known for its strong values defined in a **Corporate Aspirations Statement**. So why were these managers spending valuable retreat time looking yet again at values for their teams? For this company, a simple statement isn't enough. Values are considered a living element and evolving foundation behind every business decision. Values exploration is not a one-time event but a continuing process in which people look at what is important and how that importance is expressed in action.

A major outcome of the values retreat for a divisional management team was a Values Statement that listed the values; it also included extensive definitions of the behaviors that team members would expect to see if people were acting on each value. For example, here is the result from one team:

- **Communication**. Provide for open dialogue and the exchange of views.
- **Creativity**. We share a spirit of entrepreneurship and innovation of new ways to succeed.
- **Competency**. We embrace competency enthusiastically, always seeking to share and gain knowledge at every opportunity.
- **Teamwork**. We foster an environment that supports team members cooperating to achieve our common goals. Our motto is "We, not me."
- **Integrity**. Act in line with the beliefs of your team, organization, or other unit.
- **Personal growth**. We encourage people to take ownership of their individual learning plans, which address their personal needs and desires.

20 This example comes from our personal consulting.

- **Achievement**. Because we value achievement, we commit to quick decision-making, in which we win early and often, and to the imperative "Just do it!" with guts and courage.
- **Family.** We recognize and acknowledge the importance of our families and their contribution to our success.

Business Values in Action: The J.M. Smucker Co.

Values lists must become more than just words; they must be defined in relation to the activities of the company. One example is The J.M. Smucker Co., founded in 1897, which became a trusted brand in fruit spreads and products. While it is now a public company, the enterprise was led by a succession of family members who evolved a robust culture and guiding philosophy. Their governance structure gives family and long-term owners greater influence over policies that support their values, which are taught and emphasized by every employee. Smucker's five core values are:

- Quality
- People
- Ethics
- Growth
- Independence[21]

These values were followed implicitly under the ownership of the founding generations. Then in 1980, a non-family executive was recruited to teach and reinforce the values throughout the company. As Smucker's acquired other companies

---

21   Dennis T. Jaffe and Timothy G. Habbershon, "The Smucker Family," *Merchants of Vision* (a publication of the World Business Academy) 18, nos. 3 and 4 (June 2004).

with different cultures, they make it a point to ask those employees that enter the company through recruitment and acquisitions to know, support, and agree to live by these values. For example, in the early 2000s, when they acquired Jif (peanut butter) and Crisco (oil and shortening) from Proctor & Gamble (P&G)—a company with very different values—they explained these values and asked prospective employees to agree to them. To their surprise, Smucker's values won the enthusiastic support of most P&G acquirees.

The original values were defined in 1981 from the principles of four family generations, with the help of ethicist Rushworth Kidder. Along with the family leaders and new professional staff, the company defined an experiential training program that all employees were asked to attend. In the workshops, they learned about each value and discussed the challenges of how to apply them. They also learned that all employees would have the leaders' full support to make decisions based on the values.

The values are supported by the wisdom of four generations of Smuckers and their small Ohio town roots. Tim Smucker, the third-generation co-CEO, notes that the leaders routinely share information and power with employees to build a culture based on shared commitment and information, as well as responsibility in service of the vision of quality consumer products. Their strong brand supports their intent. Tim Smucker reports:

> This is the business and work ethic of all the Midwestern towns and communities my grandparents grew up in. Our structure today was instilled from the start. We always ran this way even when we were private. We were from a small town; everybody knows you in the town. That helps. My dad and I, and our kids, all went to the same public high school, grade schools, and my grandson is going to the same grade school. We haven't forgotten those values. This cherished legacy can only be maintained with a deep and ongoing commitment by the leadership that is continually taught and reinforced. While many companies want such values, the owners must invest, teach, and reinforce the values or they can

become stale and fall away. Many long-term family companies, through their legacy, can do this in a way that companies with more dispersed or short-term management cannot.[22]

Smucker's teaches these values to each new employee and asks that they agree to adhere to them. But they do more than that. Employees go through a training program in which they talk about what each value means and work with case examples where the values are challenged. Each employee gets a clear message that they have the freedom to make decisions based on the values, and if they do, they can expect that they will be supported.

A Lot to Be Gained

Traditionally, consensus around how to conduct the business of an organization has been achieved through strict procedures and standards of behavior under the control of supervisors. If you were in doubt and you did not act, you got approval from above. Now, with employees' greater empowerment and autonomy, they want to be less guided by rules or a supervisor and more by understanding their organization's most important values and being trusted to make their own decisions. If you judge that a decision fits the values, then it's right.

Having a common understanding is critical because different people and work groups will view values differently. While there will always be differences of emphasis and increasing diversity of values among employees, the creation of consensus about key values is an important task for any group.

22   Jaffe and Habbershon, "The Smucker Family."

CHAPTER 10

Developing and Implementing Shared Business Values

At work, as in other areas of life, people hold certain basic values and believe they act on them. But they rarely take the time to define them clearly or question them. Sometimes our most important values remain somewhat hidden from the team. Unclear, unstated, or unknown values can produce conflicts and contradictions that make people feel confused, blocked, and frustrated. Many organizational and team values are unconscious in that they lie below the surface and are not openly explored or discussed. Making the values more explicit enhances agreement and connection.

Organizational values are often based on what leaders feel is good business behavior and can be scaled across divergent priorities. Ideally, those values will be practical, lead to a profitable business, and add value to stakeholders who encounter them, as the Huber story illustrated. But too often they are vague, confusing, and even conflicting.

Organizations that want to reap the benefits of developing values need to challenge themselves to be more like Huber or Smucker. How does a company begin to empower its employees to live by and act on a set of values? Since values can be vague and unclear, enterprises must make sure that people know *what the values mean in practice*; and the company must make it clear that *their values are to be respected*. Everyone needs to be *aligned* on what they mean. This chapter looks at the development of shared organizational values.

Formal (Espoused) vs. Informal Values

A Values Statement tells you very little about how the company really operates. They can even be deceptive and misleading. Here is an example of a Values Statement from a late-twentieth-century company that grew incredibly fast and was featured on many most-admired-company lists. The values were:

- Communication
- Respect
- Integrity
- Excellence

There is some overlap with the Huber example recounted in Chapter 8. Here's the kicker: These values are from Enron, whose fall from grace and conviction of its top management led to one of the greatest corporate downfalls ever recorded!

What happened? Obviously, the values were not deeply embedded in their culture. In fact, like many companies, Enron had a public culture reflected in these values and a hidden culture of practice that was far different. The trials of the top management revealed a culture in which people made up results, hid assets in unrelated entities, did not confront their leaders, and stood by while fraud was committed. That was the operating culture, not the espoused one.

While, fortunately, few organizations have such an extreme disconnect between espoused values and actual culture, every organization has **informal**, **unspoken**, or **non-public values** that shape the actual culture of an organization. Not all these hidden values will be congruent or even in agreement with the formal public values. In fact, as demonstrated by the Enron story, many companies have informal values that are the opposite of their stated values: non-confrontation of authority, obedience, silence, secrecy, cutting corners for results, and personal agendas. People frequently act in concordance with the informal values, contradicting the desired values stated by the company. For example, an organization that values transparency may have an informal value that leaders do not share decisions or information on business results or profitability. Or that subordinates do not step up when they see their supervisors ignore a stated policy.

Sometimes, the informal culture contains values that leaders would not espouse openly, such as competing ruthlessly with your peers, making your boss look good at all costs, or making a sale no matter what you promise. These informal values can embarrass a company or, at their worst, lead people to dysfunctional and unethical actions. An informal culture that undermines or ignores their stated values can lead to serious difficulty. If the counterculture of the organization is not addressed and the expressed values are given precedence, the culture can deteriorate and look nothing like its public face.

How can these hidden counter-cultures be overcome? There is always some tension between business cultures and self-interest and the stated values. Values Statements offer a touchstone whereby visibility and public values agreement is meant to serve as a check and counteract those hidden conflicts. But a value is always an ideal, an aspiration—not always easy to live up to. A company that operates by values does not necessarily live in harmony; in fact, as we have seen in multiple case studies, acting in full alignment with values is hard and sometimes costly. A value of safety and quality, for example, may lead to missed deadlines and raising tough issues with one's leaders. Not comfortable and not easy.

Clarifying the organization's shared values and making sure employees understand what they mean—and ensuring leaders' behavior is consistent with the values—will narrow or even eliminate the gap between espoused and informal values. Clarifying values for a team and organization is an essential organizational activity, along with supporting everyone to live and work by them. When people work together to agree on what is most important to them, a shared commitment to those values can emerge.

What Values Need to Be Defined?

Table 10.A shows some of the values adopted by prominent family companies.[23]

TABLE 10.A: EXAMPLES OF COMPANY VALUES

WEGMANS	MARRIOTT	INFOSYS	COMCAST
Caring	People first	Client value	Entrepreneurial spirit
High standards	Pursue excellence	Leadership by example	Doing the right thing
Make a difference	Embrace change	Integrity & transparency	Acting with integrity
Respect	Act with integrity	Fairness	Respect for each other
Empower	Serve the world	Excellence	Giving back

MARS	GALLO	TARGET	HILTON
Quality	Integrity	More for money	Hospitality
Responsibility	Respect	Best shopping experience	Integrity
Mutuality	Humility	Healthy, happy, values team	Leadership
Efficiency	Innovation	Brighter future	Teamwork
Freedom (autonomy)	Commitment	Ethical business practices	Ownership
	Teamwork		Now (urgency)

There are two important points about these examples. First, note that these lists are all short, just five or six values per set. That brevity is key. The lesson is to focus on a few key values that you think will have the biggest impact on your organization's ability to be successful. Steer away from exhaustive lists.

Second, if you look closely at these examples, you'll see that they fall into two categories:

23 Lauren Smith-Petta and Rebecca Michael, "20 Inspirational Company Core Value Examples," *Fit Small Business*, October 2021, fitsmallbusiness.com/core-values-list/.

- **Hard values** support operational work processes, task completion, goal achievement, profitability, and business success (e.g., "high standards," "pursue excellence," and "quality"). Hard values are relatively easy to talk about and tend to be more agreed upon.

- **Soft values** support the way people interact, honor relationships, and build trust and cooperation (e.g., "respect," "executive presence," "responsibility," and "humility"). Soft values have greater variation and less clarity about what behaviors reflect them. People often have less experience with talking about these values in the workplace.

The focus of our consulting work in the 1990s was responding to requests to create "a new culture." We found this interesting because these organizations already had a culture, but it was not well articulated or usefully applied to create alignment between the culture and the policies. We worked with more than a hundred organizations, which informed the development of our Values Wheel. No matter what the industry, we found these seven core organizational values were more frequently selected:

- Integrity
- Competence
- Teamwork
- Communication
- Family
- Autonomy
- Creativity
- Personal growth

These values are connected to what have been called "soft" values, which are not traditionally thought of as being important in the work environment. But with increased attention on how a work culture supports performance, engagement, customer service and resilience, innovation, and work/life balance, soft values are now seen as essential in workplaces.

A recent study from the Center for Creative Leadership explored whether members of different work generations (ranging across almost four generations) had divergent work values. They found more agreement than difference across generations.[24] Interestingly, everyone's overwhelming top organizational value was *family*. This indicates that workers of all generations want work to be a warm, supportive place where you feel respected, comfortable, and accepted for who you are and where you can turn to others and ask for help. They want companies with family-like cultures that are consistent and dependable, no matter what their age. And workplaces are increasingly cross-generational, just like families. The many ways that employees envision work being like a family fuel some of the most important and impactful discussions about the nature of the workplace.

If people do not feel that their organization can be trusted, if there are no core values that the company stands for and is willing to struggle to uphold, then the fabric that ties people to the organization weakens. Without the so-called "soft" values emphasizing positive relationships, the willingness of people to put in extra effort, to extend themselves, and to help the organization make a difference diminishes.

Companies have begun to look to both hard and soft values together as contributing to a sense of belonging and purpose that employees seek from their work. To help organizations create a combined set of hard and soft values we offer another way to think about values (like what we did with shared family values in previous chapters, but with a few different twists). We ask our clients to list:

1. **Current values** that are evidenced in practice.

2. **Legacy values** that have likely been adapted and revised as new situations emerge.

3. **Aspirational values** that stretch the thinking about adapting to future conditions.

---

24 Jennifer Deal and Stephanie Wormington, "Tactics for Leading Across Generations," Center for Creative Leadership, March 1, 2025, https://www.ccl.org/articles/leading-effectively-articles/the-secret-to-leading-across-generations/.

Learning Journey #7 will walk you through the process of identifying the specific values in all these categories and synthesizing them into a succinct set of values to build a thriving culture.

Caveat: Check for a Potential Dark Side of Values

Even the most attractive values can turn out to have a negative impact if overused. Every value can become counterproductive; each value has had unintended consequences if overdone. Too much ice cream is no longer a treat!

As you begin to revisit and update the core values of your organization, you should be wary that traditions do not become a millstone holding your organization back. Table 10.B has examples of initial values that may have been attractive when established and the negative outcomes that can result from continuing to hold them when conditions change.

TABLE 10.B: LIGHT AND DARK SIDE OF BUSINESS VALUES

Initial Value	Impact When Overused
Lifetime employment	· Tolerance of mediocrity · Entrenched fiefdoms · No new blood to shake things up
Respect for customers Individualized service	· Neglect of new technology · Not differentiating more profitable customers · Missing new emerging markets
Assured employment for family members	· Diminishing capability and motivation · Inability to attract management talent
Loyalty prized over results	· Inability to hold people accountable for results
Traditional ways of doing things	· Lack of tolerance for new ideas · Lack of strategic planning
Family member special benefits and perks	· Depleted capital or credit to invest in the future · Not looking at profitability of company
Traditional products, services	· Aging product line, vulnerable to competitors' new products and technologies

Overuse of some values can lead to relying on values past their usefulness when we have no ongoing process of examining whether these values continue to support the intended outcome. How can these initial values be reinterpreted to fit the new business climate—to preserve what is best from the past as they innovate for changing conditions?

Applying Values Statements

Ever since Jim Collins and Jerry Porras published *Built to Last*[25] in 1994, we have been aware of the hidden power of a strong corporate-values culture, and how, when adhered to by all layers of a company, it can anchor long-term business success. Their research compared eighteen great, long-lasting companies with comparable firms that were okay but not great. Many of the long-lasting companies were, like Huber, beneficiaries of founders who embedded their values in the operations of firms that became family enterprises.

Within a few years of the publication *Built to Last*, companies all over the world came up with Values Statements that graced their walls and annual reports, but many of them found that values were only a beginning. If they did not devote resources and persistent leadership to living by the values, the values were next to useless or could even be destructive. Employees who saw their leaders not living up to their values, or even doing things that actively undermined them, could become disengaged and less committed to the organization's success.

The moral of this discussion is that you can't stop once you have a list of values or a Values Statement. The secret of making values a force for good in your organization is what you do to describe what the values mean and how you make sure there is a *shared understanding* of those values. A shared understanding should be achieved by using a collaborative process to identify and flesh out your business values.

25 James C. Collins and Jerry I. Porras, *Built to Last: Successful Habits of Visionary Companies*, 3rd ed. (Harper Business, 1994).

Check for Organizational Commitment

The process of developing and rolling out shared values does not happen quickly, nor is it without pitfalls. Above all, the organization must be committed to making sure espoused and real values are aligned, or the whole effort can fall apart. We saw the cost of a lack of full organizational commitment in a fast-growing retailer that set out to develop a corporate Values Statement. The team created to deal with this issue met regularly at the COO's house, having pizza dinners as they asked themselves what was important in the company and what should guide their future. The team members had a deep and powerful experience together as they looked at how the company could grow and develop. After several months, the resulting Values Statement was unveiled at a corporate retreat and the leadership had a positive and lively discussion before accepting it.

Next, they set up task forces, each one chaired by an executive team member and containing a cross-section of employees. The six teams each selected a key value and agreed to spend a year exploring what that value meant and what actions the company could take to actualize that value. As they looked at the proposed values—such as balancing work and family, respecting people, or career development pathways—they uncovered some deep value conflicts between what the company said and what it did (sound familiar?). Therefore, the company would have to make significant commitments to change if they truly wanted to create a culture that reflected the stated values. For example, to support work/family balance, they might not be able to expect managers to be on call twenty-four hours a day.

Sadly, the task forces faded out of existence. It seemed that the groups did not have the mandate, or the will, to confront some of the pressures of the culture itself. The values were sacrificed to the way that the organization really worked—the informal company culture.

One of the most central tasks of establishing a values-based culture is to get alignment between the informal and espoused cultures. And it needs to happen. Employees of the company we've been talking about privately expressed that what had been a source of satisfaction and motivation was now seen as an organizational failure. The cost to the company of not confronting the issues raised was that many people felt the organization, which had a reputation for using people up rather than supporting them, did not know how to respect or value its people. High turnover continues to plague this company even though it offers people challenging and well-paid work. Employees just don't feel committed to working there very long.

That example gives us a picture of the kind of values people want to see reflected in their workplaces. Such values not only support high performance but also give employees the respect to bring their whole selves to work. It's powerful to see what happens when a company or team tries to put such values into action in its own unique way.

Linking Process and Outcomes

We hope we've made clear that you need to view a Values Statement as both an outcome and the process used to achieve that outcome. It's likely your Values Statement will include a mix of hard and soft values that define not just how you want to deliver products and services to the world but also how you will treat each other internally. It will be easier for people to achieve the goals of a Values Statement if they have been involved in the process—if not to define the values, then at least to help describe what the values mean, given the decisions they face every day.

CHAPTER 11

Tending Your Values Garden

Sadly, company Values Statements are too often just popular buzzwords, taking up valuable wall space. They are a particular focus of a set of *Dilbert* cartoons, suggesting that values are a meaningless pursuit by empty-headed or hypocritical managers wasting the time of their troops. Many Values Statements are indeed empty platitudes with little or no basis in reality. At the annual retreat of one management team, we asked them to look at how well they were practicing certain values. They asked where this list came from, protesting that the values were too generic and not relevant to their company. Finally, we had to remind them that the list came from their management retreat the previous year!

That said, even if you have put effort into weaving your values into the fabric of your organization, values and purpose should not be treated as eternal; they need renewing. Defining the reasons your organization exists and how it wants to operate in the world are not one-and-done actions. They must be supported and renewed again and again with the people who matter the most: the top team, the employees, and even yourself.

How does a company inject life into their values? By treating values like a garden that needs regular tending. Creating a Values Statement is like planting a seed; it is just the first task, and more work is needed to have a flourishing garden, or, in this case, a flourishing organizational culture. Let's look at actions you can take to make sure your values stay alive and relevant in your organization.

Rethinking Leadership Development

There have been thousands of books on the qualities of effective leaders, most with a story of leadership and a list of capacities and steps to be such a leader. We have been guides and coaches for many leaders who have sought to develop a values-based organization. In that work, we have been influenced by Robert Anderson and William Adams,[26] whose model of leadership development shows how leaders systematically progress through stages of adult development, which correspond with stages of organizational development. They also link the level of leadership development to the leader's effectiveness.

For our purposes here, the important takeaway from Anderson and Adams's work is that creating a values-driven organization requires transformed leaders whose individual consciousness and mastery are linked to their inner development. The performance of an organization depends highly on the level of consciousness of its leadership.

One of the promises of leadership development is to increase capacity to respond to changing complex environments. This requires the capacity both individually and collectively to match or exceed the pace of change in the business conditions. Individual effectiveness is necessary but not sufficient. Developing leaders who can navigate complexity is a hard-to-duplicate competitive advantage. This development is not just conveying a set of skills and competencies but development of courage, compassion, consciousness, and character through the development of their own values.

The development of personal resilience is enhanced by growing through

---

26 Robert Anderson and William Adams, *Mastering Leadership: An Integrated Framework for Breakthrough Performance and Extraordinary Business Results* (Wiley, 2016).

sequential rounds of disintegration and reintegration. Growth comes from being challenged to let go of ever-changing forms of normal identity as people move through the stages of development. Many leaders approach this kind of development with reluctance and resist the tension that this kind of letting go and reformulation requires. Yet transformative change, such as the process of moving toward a values-based organization, requires all stakeholders to shift to a higher stage of development. Unless the personal transformation occurs, any improvements will be temporary. As Anderson and Adams point out, the organization will likely revert back to normal.

Making Business Values Real, Not Ornamental

We talked about the pitfalls of ornamental values in Chapter 5 when discussing shared family values. That theme is equally true here: As we've discussed, too many companies and teams create Values Statements to hang on their walls, and rather than provide a sounding board for accountability, they become artifacts of hollow intentions.

To keep your values alive and vital, you can follow the following guidelines to keep values an important part of your culture.

1. Define Behaviors

Remember the table of typical values espoused by businesses back on p. 158? The values are not so different and unique. While Values Statements are intended to highlight the virtues of each company's culture and commitments, they often contain wonderful words that sound very much alike. For that reason, many Values Statements seem bland, predictable, and similar. They make the values sound superficial and ornamental.

The lesson is that the key words used to represent values are insufficient to create commitment or change. To make them actionable they need to be anchored in behaviors that reflect that value.

- How would people act, talk, and interact if they were upholding this value?
- What happens when this value is not honored?
- What would people pay attention to if they were upholding this value?
- How will the organization reward this value?

Conversations to clarify and reinforce the shared agreement about what these values mean make the values real to people.

2. Examine What Is Rewarded in the Organization

Companies must consider how they may be making it difficult to sustain values and what they can do to minimize the tensions and conflicts. For example, one company had a value of teamwork but rewarded managers for individual results. To have an organization that sustains its values, you must ensure that behaviors that are aligned with them get acknowledged and rewarded.

3. Teach and Reinforce Values

New employees need opportunities to understand and apply the values to their work. This can start as early as in a new employee orientation process. Some questions you might want to ask of new employees include:

- Where did these values come from?
- How are they revised?
- What is the path to follow when values slip?
- Where are these values celebrated?

These values are then reinforced by their peers and managers as they go about their jobs.

Values come alive when they are used to bring attention to situations where they are being ignored. A values-based enterprise needs to demonstrate some boundaries about what is okay and what is not okay. Trust and credibility in leadership are generated if values are upheld in decision-making, hiring, firing, and the management of the work environment.

4. Stay True to Values in Hard Times

When a company prospers, it is relatively easy to act on its values. But what happens when a company faces hard times?

Values are sometimes difficult to live up to because the organization is continually changing, and some changes put great pressure on espoused values. Economic pressure to conduct layoffs to adjust to changing conditions is a prime example of business actions that will put a company's values to the test. When a company reaches a point where it cannot avoid layoffs, the question is: Can they be implemented in line with the values? How are the decisions made and acted on?

For example, over several years of working with IBM in the '90s, we saw how the decline of the company had forced it to neglect one of its core values: respect for the individual. This was variously interpreted as not firing people, not forcing people to change their ways, or not holding people accountable for poor performance. Employees were angry and upset because they felt the company was abandoning its core values.

For a time, rather than look at the need to shift their values or to set different standards of what constituted respect (e.g., could you respect people and still have layoffs or make people responsible for results?), the feelings about change went underground and were not addressed. This tended to erode IBM's second great value: being close to the customer.

The values-based company understands that major disruptions may happen, requiring the company to acknowledge how their decisions run counter to their values. It is a hard lesson, and many companies that initiate commitment to values that are difficult to live up to have them fall by the wayside, maybe not with the devastating Enron outcome, but nonetheless difficult.

What if Boeing had not swerved from its engineering excellence legacy to achieve higher profits? Could its current safety and customer failures have been prevented? The roots of the failure have been traced to a shift of leadership, which included a shift from a culture where engineering excellence was at the core, to a focus on cutting cost and profitability that led to outsourcing of parts and pressure to meet cost and time deadlines. The pursuit of safety and environmental preservation certainly adds short-term costs. The hope is that they will also lead to greater trust with customers, more positive motivation of employees, better products, and a more effective company.

Major challenges were common during the COVID pandemic and the economic shocks that accompanied it. Some companies demonstrated substantial resilience and sustained trust because they engaged in open conversations about what values they were using to make their hard choices.

Country Quest, a century-old Irish farming company founded by the Hoey brothers, faced possible closure during the COVID pandemic after successfully overcoming a huge scandal about tainted food and dealing with Brexit, which affected their major market.[27] Despite all of these challenges, the company survived, due in part to their strong values. The company was rooted in a sustainable farming model and adhered to values that included sustainability, teamwork, integrity and trust, quality, community, innovation, and giving back. They found that these core values enabled it to sustain trust and effectively collaborate with employees, suppliers, and customers throughout the crisis.

5. Link Personal and Shared Values

A classic survey by the American Management Association[28] of 1,460 managers and chief executives suggests that understanding the relationship between personal and business values can provide new leverage for corporate vitality. The survey

---

27 Eric Clinton and Stephen Browne, *Family Business Case Studies Across the World: Succession and Governance in a Disruptive Era*, Jeremy Cheng, et al., eds. (Edward Elgar Publishing, 2022).

28 Warren H. Schmidt and Barry Z. Posner, *Managerial Values and Expectation: The Silent Power in Personal and Organizational Life* (AMA Membership Publications, 1982).

provided solid evidence that shared values between the individual and the company are a major source of both personal and organizational effectiveness. When managers' values were in line with the values of their companies, their personal lives were in better shape, their approach to their jobs more optimistic, and their stress lower. The survey showed that a person's sense of what is important strongly influences his or her commitment and motivation. But be warned: This relationship, when mismanaged, can be the breeding ground for conflict and cynicism.

As we noted in earlier chapters, there does not have to be a perfect overlap between personal values and shared values of a family or organization. However, it is not just possible but essential that members of a group agree upon certain shared values of the group, which sets members' basic expectations for belonging to the group. It does not mean that everyone has only those values; rather, it clarifies the specific values expected by the group. That said, highlighting the areas where personal values align with business values can bring clarity and a sense of engagement for employees.

One power company, for example, initiated a series of focus groups to explore personal and organizational values. After looking at the core values of the organization, it looked at how these values were linked to individual values and found, for example, that employees felt pressured to find personal balance while achieving high work performance, which interfered with their commitment to the organization. Identifying this stress point led to the exploration of ways to maintain work and family balance.

When you work in an environment in which your work activities are aligned with what you consider important, the energy, motivation, desire, and commitment to fulfil even the most difficult tasks seem to increase. This ongoing process to reaffirm and recalibrate how personal values are connected to organizational values is a powerful strategy for generating engagement and releasing creativity.

6. Deal with Value Conflicts and Tensions

If we all had the same values with the same priorities, it would be easy to work together in groups. But in most teams, there is a diversity of values and beliefs. To help teams work better and make decisions that lead to commitment and action, it is necessary to see the range of values that influence the decision-making process and agree on which ones take priority.

We should all know by now that it is common to encounter tensions between values. These values conflicts provide opportunities for conversation that can bring clearer understanding and acceptance of compromises to resolve tensions.

- What if a company values honesty but also a high sales volume?
- How or when does the value of honesty influence the value of making a sale?

Many companies have been deeply wounded by such value conflicts, most often because employees did not feel they had a forum in which to explore, discuss, or revise the values. They chose loyalty over confrontation, and stayed silent, in line with the values of the hidden culture.

A values exchange and discussion are critical to clarifying the guidelines for behavior and the limits of personal responsibility. Exploring these tensions allows people to talk about the ways informal values may contradict or undermine their stated, loftier values. These discussions are difficult because many organizations place a value on avoiding conflict or not telling each other the truth when it could lead to an uncomfortable situation.

For example, a company with a strong values orientation reported that it was given a huge order from a tobacco company, with the proviso that the company eliminate its corporate no-smoking policy. The company brought this issue to every work group for discussion. They had to decide if the economic incentive the order represented was worth the values challenges it presented. Ultimately, the different work groups achieved consensus that the value was more important than the sale, and the company turned down the order rather than change its policy.[29]

---

29   This story comes from a personal communication with one of our clients.

A utilities company initiated focus groups to explore personal and organizational values. After looking at the company's core values, the groups examined how those values linked to workers' individual values. They found that employees felt pressured to sacrifice personal time in order to achieve high work performance. Identifying that stress led to exploring ways to maintain work/family balance. The values discussion brought to the surface issues that interfered with employees' commitment to the company. Crucially, these kinds of forums can bring shared respect for differing views. These forums then helped minimize or overcome the conflicts.

A company can neither anticipate nor legislate itself out of such values conflicts. What it can do, however, is discover where such conflicts exist and initiate a dialogue with those most affected. Direct engagement with the tension can often release innovative ideas for finding a path through.

Business Transformations Ignite Reexamination of Values

The pace of change today makes it necessary for organizations to continually reexamine their values. Values can be a core driver of positive evolution when there is an organizational crisis or need for renewal after a traumatic change. For example, in the 1980s, Nissan Motors faced a decline in sales and its market share. Its former president, Yutaka Katayama, decided that the pathway to the future involved going back to the company's core beliefs. He initiated a Belief Stream Process focused on building strong relationships with customers by understanding their journey and providing personalized assistance, both online and at dealerships. This approach involved the senior managers examining their core values and behaviors that supported close customer relationships. With the concept of placing customers first in mind, the managers looked at how they would change their priorities and actions.

The need to revisit values is especially important when a major corporate transformation is being considered. Major changes are not possible without a reconsideration of core values, because they underlie organizational structures, processes, and behavior. To change things permanently, you need to shift values, or the organization will tend to snap back to the way it was before—despite the attempts to change.

Evolution of the Luck Companies as a Values-Based Company

Here is a story of a hugely successful family enterprise, showing how defining values can impact a company's growth and evolution.[30] Rooted in faith, the Luck family wants to make a positive impact in the lives of people. Luck Companies is a values-based organization that enables the family to carry out their mission of igniting human potential to power possibilities for generations to come.

In 1923, Charles Luck Jr. founded a rock-quarrying company in Virginia. He never expected it to grow over the next century into the largest and fastest-growing family-owned aggregates company in the United States. Its success grew not from one person's entrepreneurialism, but from many reinventions over four generations of family ownership.

In 1995, Charlie Luck IV began the succession to leadership from his father Charles Luck III. The company had grown quickly in the mid-'90s tripling in size, employees, and geographic footprint. To deal with this size and complexity, Charlie and his leadership team decided to decentralize the company, splitting the company into regions to move decision-making closer to customers.

They did not anticipate the impact on the company's culture. The decision led to conflict over decisions, resources, and customers and began to erode the company's culture. After several years of rising conflict, and getting feedback that the culture had changed, Charlie decided to fix the leadership team. Inspired by Holt Caterpillar, another century-old family business, Luck started on a values journey.

One deep insight that moved him on his journey was that change had to

---

30 As recounted to the authors in a personal interview with Charlie Luck IV.

begin at the top, with the leaders themselves changing. As part of this work, he sought feedback from his team. He asked for feedback about his leadership and was stunned to get what he asked for—many critical comments that made it hard to work with him. He took these ideas to heart and improved his skills in listening, supporting, and encouraging input. From what he learned, he envisioned a new vision of how the company operated to achieve its growth goals. It was based on defining the values and culture of the company so that everyone had greater responsibility and engagement. This called for a new set of values about how they work together as a company, modeled in part on Ken Blanchard and Michael O'Connor's *Values-Based Management*[31] to develop the stewardship skills of everyone in the company.

It was a total redesign of how the company operated to begin the new century and third generation of family leadership. With his leadership team, they clarified their organizational values:

- Commitment
- Integrity
- Creativity
- Leadership

This is the behavior that the leaders wanted to see. How were they going to make that happen? He knew that they couldn't just demand such new behavior. They had to go first, modeling what they expected from others. Starting with the leadership team, and continuing to the front line of the business, the organization embarked on an intense period of self-discovery and development, putting Values-Based Leadership into action at every level.

This was not a theoretical activity; the work totally changed how the company operated. Over the years, the company found that as the business's culture grew more aligned, the business's outcomes improved. For example, the company saw:

31   Ken Blanchard and Michael O'Connor, *Managing by Values* (Berrett-Kohler, 2003).

- Improved customer loyalty and key account retention through integrity and commitment toward anyone the company met.
- Increased innovation by focusing and embracing creativity throughout the company.
- Better efficiency and safety through an unwavering commitment to a best-in-class safety program.
- Acquisition advantages by gaining respect as an industry leader for operating with integrity as a care value in everyday operations.

Additionally, the company began to hear stories of associates taking their newly found leadership skills home. Examples poured in of better parenting, stronger marriages, and better people at work and at home.

To make this transformational change toward fast growth and innovation, they knew they needed to invest in training and development. Many efforts marked the roll-out of the Vision for a Value-Based Organization. Many steps were taken to make this a reality. From their intention came a commitment and some foundational changes in how they worked as a company, along the path to their ambitious expansion:

- Monthly Values Program. Year long, starting from the top, with groups of forty being trained.
- Rituals. For example, in the beginning of the values journey, the company began incorporating values in action stories into company meetings. meeting starts with sharing values stories.
- Incorporation of values into performance review.
- Value training curriculum.
- Bonuses based on values and Values-Based Leadership.
- Values coaches in the field, focused on supporting managers and front-line associates.

- Quarterly values program for all staff.

- Mentoring program, from top moving down.

- Ongoing officer development and coaching.

- New employee surveys and interviews focused on values.

- New officer incentive plan tied to self-development.

All of these made the values a focus and allowed the culture to become very different, as all levels of associates became more active and involved. A sense of new energy and excitement spread across every business unit and work group.

But as with every major change, there were unexpected challenges. Charlie had a life-threatening illness that took him away for a time. A huge recession in 2008 affected their operations, to the degree that they had to reduce staff. But the effort did not diminish, and the effects showed on the business results. The growth happened faster than expected. Despite setbacks, the efforts continued. Under Charlie's leadership, the company created six five-year strategic planning periods spanning from 2000 to 2025. These strategic planning windows have been instrumental in the growth and evolution of the company and recently culminated in expansion into new markets and communities within Virginia, North Carolina, South Carolina, and Georgia, with new locations across the Southeast, including the largest acquisition in company history.

During his time as CEO, the company has been recognized nationally as a leader in safety and environmental stewardship. In addition, under Charlie's leadership, the engagement and enablement of Luck Companies' associates have been recognized as some of the strongest in the United States and globally, as a result of a twenty-year focus on igniting human potential through Values-Based Leadership, and eventually founding a nonprofit leadership institute—InnerWill—to teach other leaders how to build values-based organizations that ignite the potential in people.

Today, Charlie's son Richard is leading the company. Always drawn to his grandfather's vision of "We care," and inspired by his dad's vision of igniting human potential, Richard believes the greatest impact he can have is supporting the people of Luck Companies. He is focused on developing a scalable company and culture where people come first and associates perform in roles that invigorate their purpose, passions, and competencies.

Keeping Your Values Relevant

Developing a Values Statement that reflects how your organization wants to exist in the world is a major achievement that deserves celebration. Having clear values and understanding how they are reflected in behavior creates a foundation of shared commitment and focus.

As we've said many times, living by values is not easy; it is a constant process of thoughtful reflection followed by making tough choices and taking strong action. It requires a willingness to talk about the difference between espoused values and hidden, unspoken values. These tensions will continue to be challenging and are indications of a need to focus on cultural alignment.

Values and their application must be nurtured as you would nurture plants in a garden. Neglect them and they will die. Tend them and they will flourish, and your organization will reap the benefits you sought by working on values in the first place.

Action Steps for Creating a Values-Based Culture

We have covered a lot of ground showing how challenging it is to build an operational and workable values framework for a company. Too many companies just rush to action, with the top leaders or the company board quickly proposing the values. This can lead to nice public relations results but rarely does much for the company. To be of real transformational benefit, the identification and consolidation of values requires time and resources and may increase conflict before alignment can be reached.

This Learning Journey provides a framework and sequence of phases for bringing values into a company culture. This is not a simple tweaking of a culture but represents an investment to support a major realignment of strategy. This is a generic overview of how values development or renewal can proceed. Doing it correctly will entail a significant investment of time and resources over a period that can measure in years, with a lot of back and forth and a high level of engagement across the company.

The steps we describe here are our recommended sequence, but you do not necessarily have to do them in this exact order. In fact, some steps may overlap or take more time than expected. But it's important

CONTINUED ↓

to have clear, top-level leadership attention to keep moving forward, no matter what other distractions and unexpected events intervene.

These steps were developed and used in several transformational change engagements. They were refined and formed into a methodology in an intensive engagement with a global consulting firm to provide guidance for global large-scale transformation projects, such as shifting manufacturing, rebuilding national educational systems, and upgrading systems and processes with technology.

The following steps are presented in our book *Getting Your Organization to Change* (Crisp, 1999). Please understand there is no method that fits all situations. We are providing the framework for you to design and sustain these transformations by connecting leadership and organizational values alignment.

Tip: Use a neutral facilitator for the process.

Just as we advised for family groups who are developing a Values Statement, it's a good idea to use a neutral facilitator to lead you through the activities described in this Learning Journey. Doing so can help ensure that all voices are heard and conflicts are resolved productively.

Step 1: Convene a values task force.

To clarify organizational values, gather a team that represents both the current and the younger, emerging leadership. This task force is responsible for designing and continuous refining the values so they support and energize the change process.

The task force is made up of people who are known to be innovative, respected, and persistent. These four to six people will be the stewards of this cross-functional process, connecting multiple groups of stakeholders to consolidate a shared Values Statement.

Step 2: Understand and celebrate your legacy values.

Remember your organization already has values. While the elders, owners, and key leaders may remember and have personal relationships with the early founders and know the history and legacy values, most employees came more recently and have no idea of the company's origins. It is helpful to gather stories, correspondence, artifacts, policies, and documents that showcase how the values of the early leaders were used in the founding of the company. Explore ways to share these with the organization in celebrations, websites, and all-hands meetings/online gatherings. For example, Luck, Smucker, Huber, and other successful values-based companies share stories that highlight key decisions, pivots, and challenges that were successfully navigated by focusing on the company's values.

There's a famous business myth about an employee who took a huge risk that failed miserably. Reporting the disastrous results to the founder, the employee expected to be summarily fired. He submitted his resignation. The founder responded, "Fire you? We just invested a huge amount to educate you, so we expect you to learn and contribute great things in the future." This story illustrates the value of having respect for employees and supporting those who take risks and present new ideas.

Stories can be added to strategic briefings, discussions at board meetings, and other events to connect the company's values to past success. They become a source of pride and engagement as they become part of the fabric of the culture. We have seen powerful dialogues that bring in retired and influential historical figures to share their stories of how their values guided their success.

Many companies also commission company histories. Others have archives and even have company museums. These can provide a great starting point for a values initiative. They show what the company stood for, why the company has been successful, and why employees want to work there. The employees want to hear the stories; they provide the background for creating the pride and energy needed for values work.

Step 3: Connect values to current challenges.

After sharing stories and history, the next phase involves engaging employees to identify current challenges and explore how these values could be used to provide competitive differentiation.

This stage is very public and open, and the task force must take care that everyone understands that these sessions are to generate ideas and that there will be no decisions, criticism, or arguments. At this stage, the goal is to provide a place for employees to offer their views on how they see the company's values being used to deal with challenges in the current environment. Analysis and focusing will come later.

McDonald's initiated this kind of process when they shifted their focus to include more emphasis on sustainability, with attention to climate action, responsible sourcing, reducing waste, and transitioning to sustainable packaging. The aim was to create a positive impact on people, communities, and the planet. In order to connect their vision to their values, they gathered a task force to engage their global organizations in discussions about the company values. They began with the restaurant crews. They created discussion guides for each value and held a "15-minute huddle" each week to talk about the following questions.

- How have our values been part of our current success/resilience?
- How do our values spark quality?
- How could the leadership strengthen the connection between the values and policies and practices?
- Where do they see these values in action?

Some additional ways organizations have engaged employees in seeing the values in action include:

- initiating a confidential survey to collect input on areas where the values are being seen and areas where there are gaps. These themes could be validated in cross-functional conferences.

- organizing a series of cross-functional conferences within the organization to identify how values have been part of creating successful strategies, policies, or decisions.

- taking the themes from these conferences to engage and extend groups of customers, stakeholders, board members, and community members to identify how they see the values in action.

Step 4: Consolidate and organize the main values themes.

The task force can then consolidate what was learned into a condensed version of the themes that occurred from the discussions, surveys, and meetings. These reports can be used to update the current values and point out emerging values that can be incorporated when revising the company's vision for the future.

This refreshed set of values can then inform the strategy to match this future vision. These two processes can be done alongside one another, but it's best to keep the strategic planning process and the values clarification separate until they are complete: They can be combined at the end.

Step 5: Share and discuss the draft Values Statement.

Release the draft and share the thinking behind the statement with employees. Share the origins and considerations that went into it. Ask for feedback about wording, ask what's great about it, what is missing, and what might be important. The task force then makes revisions and sets up a process for formal validation by the leadership team. Celebrate the outcome of producing this new Values Statement.

Sometimes this step is the end of the values creation project. However, our experience is that this is just the midpoint of the process. Now begins a new round of applying the values to current situations. This is where the values become real and actionable, as opposed to vague and often ambiguous aspirations.

Step 6: Connect the new values to current work challenges.

Starting with the top- and second-level leadership team, then with teams from each division or business unit, convene workshops to get examples of how the values are applied in action. For each value, gather stories in which the value was utilized (maybe in challenging circumstances). Collect examples of what it means and where it comes into play. This is done for each value, with the intention of gathering materials for an experiential training that can be used for engaging teams, new employees, and the leadership as they apply and align the values with the work. The purpose is to create a forum in which the values are introduced and where employees can discuss times when the values might be invoked, and how to handle such situations. These values trainings become a regular part of employee learning.

The values are discussed at team-building sessions and annual meetings and are used to reward and celebrate individuals and teams that become "values champions" by applying the values in a contentious or difficult situation. Incorporating these activities ensures that instead of being ornamental, the values become real and part of the actual working culture of the organization. They become values in practice, rather than aspirations or good intentions. They are also recognized as serious by all levels of the organization, especially for decisions where an employee may diverge from regular policies or the chain of authority. If this regular reinforcement and discussion does not happen, the values may lose salience or fall into disuse.

The Values Journey Continues . . .

We come to the end of our workbook, but it is only a rest stop in your jour-ney. You are now familiar with the importance of clarifying and refreshing personal, family, and organizational values. If you have been with us through these pages, you know that living by your values is a nice aspiration, but if you want to live a values-centered life yourself, and with your family and at work, you must be prepared for an ongoing engagement. You need to revisit your values at key times of change in your personal life and engage your organizations and communities in taking stock of how your actions line up with the values you have set out to follow. As we said early on, your life is a work of art, and you are the artist.

From the first steps of defining your deep values and purpose to putting them into action, renewing, and updating them, you must be thoughtful and vigilant. The concepts and Learning Journeys in this book can help you along the way, but only if you commit to putting in the effort and meeting the challenge of setting your values in action.

While there are solitary moments of reflection along the way, values work is not only a solitary pursuit, even if you are just working on your personal values. You can get encouragement, guidance, and inspiration from those who are important to you. Living by your values is a journey best done with others—your family, friends, colleagues, and work associates. You and they will share some values and join together for projects and pursuits that give pleasure and meaning to your life.

This book is not one that you can run through quickly and finish soon. It is a "do-ing" book that asks you to step away and reflect and try things out at each stage of the journey. We hope that you will keep it nearby and refer to it when you feel a challenge arising to what you deeply believe and aspire to. There are actions and choices you will want to revisit. There will be times when you want to renew and rethink what you had assumed was settled.

Values are the core cells that make you who you are, but unlike biological cells, they are not fixed and can be reshaped and refashioned as new possibilities and aspirations surface.

Values are a journey, not a destination. We hope this guide has been helpful to you in making them a value-building reality in your life.

Best wishes,
Cynthia and Dennis, your guides

Acknowledgments

Our values work extends over more than thirty years, and we have been guided, assisted, and supported by so many wonderful people. We want to thank so many people who have read and reread numerous versions of these materials, introduced them in their work, had courageous conversations about values tensions, and held the space for people to talk about what matters in their lives.

We appreciate the many advisors who have introduced this tool to their practices, consultants who have added it to their leadership development sessions, organizations that have brought values into everyday practice, and families who have clarified legacy and emerging values to guide them in decision-making about the future.

Family Business Colleagues: Larry Allman, Stacy Allred, Pat Armstrong, Caroline Bailey, Dave Barnard, Peter Begalla, David Bork, Arne Boudewyn, Jeremy Cheng, Mike Cole, Stacy Conrad, Jim Coutre, Leslie Dashew, Martim De Arantes Oliviera, Katherine Dean, Peter Evans, Jim Grubman, Sara Hamilton, Amy Hart-Clyne, Barbara Hauser, Jay Hughes, Michele Mikeska Jaffe, Dirk Junge, Alejandro Mendez, Madeline Levine, Richard Milroy, Asin Nurani, Joe Paul, Sisi Provost, Christian Stewart, Amelia Renkert-Thomas, Kirby Rosplock,

Laurent Roux, Wendy Sage-Howard, Richa Singh, Michael Warszawski, David Werdiger, Marc Zussman

Changeworks Colleagues: Mary Diggins, Arif Hasyim, Marcia Ruben, Glenn Tobe, Rebecca Turner, Janet Schatzman

Supportive Family and Friends: Kai Jaffe, Oren Jaffe, Anya Lane, Rosa Lopez-Jaffe, Colton Scott, Sue Scott

Banyan Colleagues: Karen Dillon, Nick DiLoreto, Rob Lachenauer, Stephan Roche, Michele Shafer, Judy Lin Walsh, Sam Gant.

Associations and Organizations that nurtured our work: African Family Business Network, Aspen Family Business Group, Collaboration for Family Flourishing, Family Business Network, Family Office Exchange, Fielding Graduate University, Kaiser Permanente, Presidio Graduate School, Pitcairn Family Office, Purposeful Planning Institute, R360, Tiger 21, Ultra High Net Worth Institute, Young Presidents Organization, Wells Fargo

Additional Resources

Interested in taking your *Living Your Values* journey further?
Visit our website to learn more and access the following resources.

THE VALUES EDGE 2.0 TOOLKIT

This is a complete toolkit for groups and facilitators, coaches, and leaders to guide others through in-person values exploration using our signature values card decks and pyramid displays.

‣ Includes 8 reusable values card decks, pyramid display cards, a 100-page facilitator guide, and a 35-page participant workbook for structured group facilitation.

‣ Helps explore legacy, current, and emerging values using the Values Wheel for alignment in strategy, succession, and culture.

‣ Offers optional two-hour training helps you experience the process and confidently design your own sessions.

ONLINE VALUES EXPLORATION

This is a quick access path to creating a Personal Values Pyramid, identifying key priorities and Values Drivers. Emerge with a clear set of values to help you make important decisions, strengthen relationships, define your purpose, and explore your values with others.

‣ Self-paced interactive online process to define core values.

‣ Clarify your life purpose and direction. Uncover neglected areas to enhance your growth and development.

‣ Certificate of current values priorities, aspirational values, and Values Drivers.

VALUES WORKSHOPS AND TALKS

This is your invitation to bring values work to life—together. Host a live, interactive session for your family, team, or organization. Identify shared values, reduce conflict, and align for the future.

‣ Live, interactive sessions for families, teams, and organizations to identify and align personal and shared values.

‣ Designed for settings like family meetings, team offsites, leadership retreats, and cross-generational planning.

‣ Supports strategic alignment, trust-building, and culture blending during transitions like mergers or growth.

Index

About the Authors

CYNTHIA SCOTT, PHD, MPH, is a San Francisco-based executive coach and advisor to leaders about transformational culture change, global leadership development, and behavioral resilience. As a founder of Changeworks Global and an executive for Saatchi & Saatchi S, Lee Hecht Harrison, Towers Perrin, and Presidio Graduate School, Dr. Scott has translated her experience into writing books and designing capability development programs, assessment tools, and models to enable people to become creative sources of resilience for their teams and organizations. She is the author of fourteen books, among them:

- *Living Your Values*
- *Leadership for Sustainability and Change*
- *Take This Work and Love It*
- *Getting Your Organization to Change*
- *Rekindling Commitment*
- *Managing Organizational Change*
- *Organizational Mission, Vision, and Values*

Dr. Scott has a BA degree in Anthropology from U. C. Berkeley, Regents Scholar, an MPH in health planning from the University of Michigan, and a

PhD clinical psychology from the Fielding Graduate University. She is a professor emeritus of Leadership at Presidio Graduate School and has been recognized as an Outstanding Faculty member, having served over 1,400 MBA and MPA students in ten years.

CONNECT WITH CYNTHIA:

cscott@cynthiascott.net
www.changeworkslab.com
www.regenerativechangelab.com

DENNIS T. JAFFE, PHD, is a San Francisco-based advisor to families about family business, governance, wealth, and philanthropy. He is a senior research fellow at Banyan Global Family Business Advisors. Dr. Jaffe is the author of:

- *Borrowed from Your Grandchildren*
- *Finding Her Voice and Leaving a Legacy*
- *Cross Cultures*
- *Stewardship in Your Family Enterprise*
- *Working with the Ones You Love*

The Family Firm Institute awarded Dr. Jaffe the 2017 International Award for service, and in 2005 he received the Beckhard Award for service to the field. In 2020, he was awarded a special commendation as an individual thought leader in the field of wealth management by the Family Wealth Report. He has a BA degree in philosophy, an MA in management, and a PhD in sociology, all from Yale University. Dr. Jaffe is a professor emeritus of organizational systems and psychology at Saybrook University in San Francisco.

CONNECT WITH DENNIS:

djaffe@dennisjaffe.com
www.dennisjaffe.com

www.ingramcontent.com/pod-product-compliance
Lightning Source LLC
Chambersburg PA
CBHW081240220326
41597CB00023BA/4225